THE LOYALTY LEAP

THE LOYALTY LEAP

Turning Customer Information into Customer Intimacy

BRYAN PEARSON

PORTFOLIO / PENGUIN

PORTFOLIO / PENGUIN
Published by the Penguin Group
Penguin Group (USA) Inc., 375 Hudson Street,
New York, New York 10014, U.S.A.
Penguin Group (Canada), 90 Eglinton Avenue East, Suite 700,
Toronto, Ontario, Canada M4P 2Y3
(a division of Pearson Penguin Canada Inc.)
Penguin Books Ltd, 80 Strand, London WC2R 0RL, England
Penguin Ireland, 25 St. Stephen's Green, Dublin 2, Ireland
(a division of Penguin Books Ltd)
Penguin Books Australia Ltd, 250 Camberwell Road, Camberwell,
Victoria 3124, Australia
(a division of Pearson Australia Group Pty Ltd)
Penguin Books India Pvt Ltd, 11 Community Centre, Panchsheel Park,
New Delhi – 110 017, India
Penguin Group (NZ), 67 Apollo Drive, Rosedale, Auckland 0632,
New Zealand (a division of Pearson New Zealand Ltd)
Penguin Books (South Africa) (Pty) Ltd, 24 Sturdee Avenue,
Rosebank, Johannesburg 2196, South Africa

Penguin Books Ltd, Registered Offices:
80 Strand, London WC2R 0RL, England

First published in 2012 by Portfolio / Penguin,
a member of Penguin Group (USA) Inc.

1 3 5 7 9 10 8 6 4 2

LIBRARY OF CONGRESS CATALOGING IN PUBLICATION DATA
Pearson, Bryan.
The loyalty leap : turning customer information into customer intimacy / Bryan Pearson.
p. cm.
Includes bibliographical references and index.
ISBN 978-1-59184-491-4 (hardback)
1. Customer loyalty. 2. Customer relations. 3. Marketing—Data processing.
4. Market surveys. I. Title.
HF5415.525.P43 2012
658.8'343—dc23
2012000414

Printed in the United States of America
Set in Warnock Pro
Designed by Lucy Albanese

To the LoyaltyOne associates, past and present,
whose leadership, passion, and effort
inspired this book in so many ways.

CONTENTS

INTRODUCTION

From Customer Information to Customer Intimacy: What's Behind the Curtain?

It is a vexing situation for business leaders that one of our most valuable assets is also the least likely to be quantified. But how does a chief accountant measure what inspires a person? It's hard enough to identify our best customers, let alone know what moves them to choose one brand over another.

If I asked you about your company's profitability, you'd be able to produce income statements and quarterly reports. If I asked about assets and capital expenditures you'd refer to the balance sheet and cash flow statement. It's black and white. But what if I asked how loyal your customers are? Could you back up the answer with a definitive formula or measure? As consumer choices proliferate, it is one of the most important questions we face.

In an age where people are joining more loyalty programs than ever before, with more than 2 billion memberships in the United States alone, we still have no hard evidence of their true underlying commitment to our brands and services.[1] Sure, they may visit one of our locations regularly, but is that because they actually go out of their way to do business with us, or because there is no better alternative? Add to this the accelerating sophistication (and affordability) of technology, which empowers consumers to make highly educated purchase decisions in moments, and you have tremendously challenging market conditions to overcome.

Yet as companies struggle to determine how loyal their customers are in this increasingly competitive and fickle market, the loyalty marketing industry, which is worth tens of billions of dollars, is growing dramatically on a global scale. For those closest to the industry, this is not a surprise. The fundamentals of loyalty marketing are relevant to everyone from retailers to credit card companies, from service companies to health care and now even to governments.

True loyalty marketing transcends the programmatic experience that occupies the wallets of most consumers—make a purchase, earn a few points. The best loyalty marketing leaders have come to understand that their programs are a way to connect with customers on a level elevated beyond mere transactions. The customer information and insights that arise from these loyalty programs is the fuel required to empower a new competitive platform.

Today I lead an organization, LoyaltyOne, that is dedicated to the scientific pursuit of unlocking the secrets that motivate consumer behavior. It's an organization that brings sixteen hundred people to work every day with a single goal: improving the way consumers interact with and experience the services of our company and those of our clients.

Together we've been shaping the loyalty industry over the last twenty years, and in ways you might not expect.

At LoyaltyOne we have developed programs that have, over twenty years, affected the behavior of more than 120 million people around the world. We also operate the AIR MILES Reward Program, the largest loyalty program in Canada, where we work with two decades of customer spending information to bring incremental value to more than one hundred leading brands. In Canada, our brand has higher penetration than any credit card, higher usage than any laundry soap, and higher retention than any wireless service.

Just as important, our customer relationships are built on trust, and we see the net benefit in customer engagement. We churn out service offers and targeted messaging as much as any other marketer, but our customers are so receptive to our communications that to date, only ten thousand of our ten million active households have opted out of receiving targeted marketing from the program. To put it another way, 99.99 percent of our customers actively agree to receive our marketing communications.

This occurs despite the ongoing debate over consumer privacy, which is very much alive in our markets. So why are our customers going against the grain? They do so because of an implicit understanding between us: They demand that their unique needs be met, and we meet those needs. The more advanced our capabilities, the more refined consumer expectations become. So as in any dynamic relationship, we have to raise our game to meet these refined expectations, and we need the rigor of data and customer management to do it. Success is the result of understanding our customers' needs, respecting their privacy, constructing some of their experiences, and having the tools for the job.

It started for me in 1992, when I accepted an offer to become the twenty-fifth employee of a company launching a new loyalty program in Canada formed around what we called "coalition loyalty." This is a rewards plan involving dozens or hundreds of companies that enables their customers to earn and then redeem a common currency (points or miles) with *any* of the program's sponsors;

these may include grocery stores, gas stations, and other retailers. The consumers' spending information, stored in a tightly held database, enables the sponsoring companies to better understand their customers so they can deliver more relevant offers.

At the time the notion was as abstract as it was revolutionary. I left a flourishing career in packaged goods, making both my wife and my banker think I was crazy. No one really understood what we were trying to do, and our early sales meetings were like university seminars in the science of customer behavior. But almost twenty years later Canada's AIR MILES Reward Program stands as an international benchmark for retail loyalty and customer management. Not only did we build a winning business, but our unique approach to mining personal customer information and shopping data has yielded superior returns for our partners while giving back $500 million each year to our Canadian members.

That said, customer management is an inexact science. In this book I'll be sharing some of the hard-fought lessons we've learned and methods refined through the years of test-and-learn activities. By sharing our voyage of discovery, and the way we add value to our partner businesses, I hope to show how customer information and making the Loyalty Leap will carry your business to a new strategic plane, one where the customer really is the center of your business purpose.

The Path from Medicine to Marketing

Although I've spent the recent decades of my life in the loyalty business, I certainly didn't set out to define my career by helping companies create value with consumer information. Rather, I was going to become a doctor, a pursuit that promised to fulfill my curiosity about how things work, and it was something I had wanted to do since I was ten years old. Both my parents were doctors, so you can imagine that science, medicine, and the function of the human body were popular topics of conversation and education around our house. My brothers and I remember ad hoc lessons conducted at the kitchen table with something that would later become dinner; my father carefully dissected a beef kidney to explain its anatomy and physiology. From an early age I had an unnatural predisposition for forensics, pathology, and clinical manifestations. These lessons fed my natural curiosity and were my passion.

So I set off to Queen's University determined to pursue a career in medicine or science. During the summers I ran my own little businesses to raise money, painting houses and doing other odd jobs. Unexpectedly I awoke a slumbering but healthy entrepreneurial streak, along with a fascination for the mechanics of business. Eventually these interests lured me away from medicine and I began to study business full-time. While completing my MBA, this interest was further refined to the pursuit of marketing, and I took my first job in product management at the Quaker Oats Company. Yet while the experience I gained there solidified my understanding of marketing as a practice, it left me hungry and unsatisfied. I loved the idea of marketing, but the practice at the time seemed closer to voodoo than to the scientific method I had spent so many years learning. For one thing, consumer goods companies operate in a closed system, selling to retailers but not gaining any real consumer relationships, because the data resided with the merchant.

I remember one meeting with our advertising agency; the agenda was to set the right level of spending for our next marketing campaign. The agency executives had arrived with a recommendation to spend an additional $2 million on media, with an argument describing why it would build market share. When I asked them to quantify how that would increase sales—a reasonable request—there was a lot of awkward shifting in chairs but almost nothing in the way of solid information to support their recommendation. I was a lost ball in the high weeds. The industry labored under the simple supposition that more media equaled more sales, and media planning was a function of how much a brand could budget rather than an exercise in understanding the dynamics of consumer purchase behavior. In my pursuit of science, I knew I had a long road to travel.

After three years at Quaker Oats, I was lucky enough to segue into the software sector, where I finally gained meaningful exposure to the world of direct marketing. It was as though someone had pushed a quantification button in my brain. Here was an entire stream of marketing in which scientific principles ruled. Let's be clear: This is not the stuff of advanced decision science, but even in the pioneering days of target marketing you had research involving control groups to determine baseline consumer behavior, and it was possible to actually measure incremental shifts. I was hooked, and I've spent the rest of my life in the pursuit of "measured marketing"—marketing based on the measurement of actual consumer behavior—finally landing in a world where I was able to frame an entire business around the creation of strategies based on deep insights into consumers.

From Marketer to Myth Buster

In the early days of loyalty marketing I often thought my business card should read GRAND ILLUMINATOR OR MYTH BUSTER. It was amazing how uninformed most companies really were about their customers and how these customers used their services. Retailers spent their time looking at traffic counts and average basket size, with the enlightened ones taking down license plate numbers in the parking lot, so that they could map out where customers lived and determine their catchment areas by store. Fliers were distributed based on where the store manager lived, the brand was defined by the preferences of the management team, and prices were hiked up or cut down based on customer complaints.

When I first began sharing the behavioral insights from our loyalty card database with senior executives at our partner companies, the lightbulbs started to blink. For the first time these executives had indisputable evidence of shopping patterns. They finally understood the spending habits and diverse profiles of the consumers who shopped at their stores. *Moms with kids* was not one segment; it was at least a dozen. Our partners could communicate directly to their customers based on what they spent and how often they shopped. Spend and frequency models are the price of entry in today's world. But a little data went a long way twenty years ago in helping to break down the walls of misconception about the way consumers interacted with businesses.

In my role as data myth buster, the truth wasn't always well received. I recall one presentation on consumer insights during which a rather skeptical retail executive scoffed at the results, attempting to discredit the data, as it didn't align with his strategic direction. Thinking he could fight numbers with numbers, he asked: "So, how many of our customers were captured in this study, two hundred, five hundred, or one thousand?" I told him it was 689,371. "It's based on the actual shopping habits of your consumers over the past twelve months." There was a long and awkward silence, and one I should have treasured more, because it signaled the moment that the world changed for our partner. We got past that rather uncomfortable meeting, and over time I helped him spearhead an initiative that fundamentally changed their go-to-market strategy. The happy ending is that we now have a twenty-year legacy of creating insights and value-added programs with this client, and a longitudinal view of its customers that is unique.

So here I am, leading a group of sixteen hundred passionate people who help our global partners maximize the value of their loyalty programs and the customer data they contain across almost every imaginable consumer category. Our flagship brand continues to be AIR MILES, with more than 70 percent of Canadian households actively collecting reward miles and responding to offers across every marketing communications channel, from print to online. We have information stemming from more than $80 billion of Canadian spending, and we set the pace for the most active loyalty market in the world.

Despite the press coverage about a world seemingly obsessed with consumer privacy, we seem to have obtained the trust—or, at minimum, the consent—of our customers to leverage their information and build mutually beneficial relationships with our retail and service partners. From the very beginning we were maniacal about balancing the business interests of our clients and those of our shared customers, recognizing that we had been entrusted with the best customer file for the most prominent brands in the country.

Taking Our Lessons, and Intimacy, on the Road

So what lessons can be learned from AIR MILES? Canada exhibits all the same competitive drivers as any other mature retail market in the developed world, and it represents what will come in emerging markets. If data-driven decisions deliver a consistently positive return on investment and customer experience in a market with just over 30 million people, imagine the benefits in India with 1.2 billion and counting.

My goal in this book is to give you an insider view of how we build trust with consumers, and to trace that experience back to the judicious use of consumer data, as the next frontier in strategic differentiation. Some industry leaders have embraced customer management but others just mouth the words, waiting for some ethereal notion, like the 360-degree view of the customer, to materialize out of their enterprise-data warehouse. All CEOs, who are now facing a recessionary decade (or more), will require the skills to sit up and take notice of their customers and to push their organizations beyond quarterly earnings for shareholder value to build lasting customer value.

My deep desire is to shift the conversation within your company from the analytics group (buried in the bowels of most organizations) to the boardroom, and eventually to the front lines—where the consumer lives. More specifically, this book should provide you with the tools to abandon the conquest mentality, where acquisition is king. Customers can only be acquired, churned, and reactivated so many times before they tire of your brand. There is a proven marketing equation in which customers willingly share information with you in the expectation of being better served and valued during future transactions. Capitalizing on that equation is our business responsibility. You can be a large multinational or a single-site operator; the principles and approaches are the same.

Whether you operate a business or are simply curious about how marketers approach customer information, my goal is to demystify some of what goes on behind the scenes. Consumers have the right to expect more, and the valuable information that is shared with companies should be used to build a more satisfying experience for the consumer.

What You Can Expect

In the remainder of this book I'll show you the trends that are shaping the rapidly changing world of customer-experience marketing and explore how some of the most successful companies are navigating this world. There are powerful forces that are transforming marketing today. We are operating in a period of rapid innovation in which leveraging customer information can create a significant strategic advantage for a company. Today's consumer is well aware of how organizations are trying to track his or her activities, and yet many data-based marketers are failing to capitalize fully on the expectations of the consumer. They are all making the same mistakes in how they manage customer data, and this is contributing to frustration, and in some cases concern, about the issue of consumer privacy.

The key, of course, is in finding the most responsible and fair way to capitalize on this information. The reality is that while many leaders espouse a customer-first approach, they are sitting on a wealth of unrealized value for the consumer in the data they possess. Using this data as the foundation on which to build more intimate customer relationships can be a vital source of profitable growth for any company, in any industry, because intimacy is achieved first through customer loyalty. But launching a loyalty program is not the real solution. Loyalty programs are an elegant way to establish an information exchange and communication platform with your customers, but it's what you do with the program and the embedded data that really defines the winners and the losers.

This is very important, because loyalty is not one-dimensional. Instead, as I'll explore, loyalty can exist on several planes, including behavioral and emotional ones, the latter of which promises to secure the consumer's meaningful, long-term engagement with your brand. Among the building blocks critical to securing emotional loyalty are what I call the Three Rs of Loyalty—Rewards, Recognition, and Relevance. But it is primarily relevance, and how you motivate the entire organization to use customer data to deliver on your brand experience, that is instrumental to emotional loyalty.

Due to its weighty role, I believe that relevance possesses its own unique complexity. In fact, I will submit that there are four behavior-based approaches to creating relevance—spatial, temporal, individual, and cultural—and it is by recognizing the consumer's relationship to these characteristics that we have the recipe to establish relevance. But this customer recognition, and the ensuing connection, requires a carefully calculated communications strategy.

So many forward-leaning strategies and tactics apply. For instance, I love the thought of equation-based marketing and how that can help structure the marketing approaches of an organization. We have the emerging concept of using hope rather than fear to inspire consumer behavior and realize untapped opportunities. Then there is the groundbreaking practice of Enterprise Loyalty, which means committing the entire organization to the pursuit of data for the sole purpose of elevating the consumer experience in unexpected places, from the in-box to the aisle.

Such heightened philosophies require organizationwide transformations and an evolution from being a company that is obsessed with the product, or with simply using its tools to take advantage of opportunities as they arise, to being a company committed completely to the customer. Such endeavors demand that all communications and interactions be designed with the customer first, whether through the ever more complex multichannel marketing or social networking, or in how we enable our frontline associates to really understand and provide better service to our customers.

In the end we return to the critical question of privacy. Worries about consumer privacy are not going to waltz away, and yet our ability to capitalize on loyalty will only be enabled if we can continue to build trust in a data-based exchange of value with the customer. Based on the experience of my company there's clearly a way to accomplish this, and there's a definitive path that will gain the confidence of both consumers and the regulatory bodies and advocacy groups that are intent on protecting consumers.

All of these grand concepts, intertwined to form a thriving organism of consumer trust, are required to make the Loyalty Leap.

I have the unique privilege to be a loyalty marketer in one of the most exciting times in marketing. I have also dedicated more than twenty years of my business career to maximizing the value of data and transforming it into relevant communications that encourage long-term customer loyalty. This book will, for the first time, take you behind the curtain and show you how it is done.

CHAPTER 1

Four Forces Are Reshaping Marketing: Can You Ride the Wave of Change?

The north shore of Oahu is known as the surfboarders' paradise, but there are waves so great that they exceed the skills of even the most experienced surfers. These waves, some larger than fifty feet, were long a force that both beckoned to and bedeviled the best athletes in the world. These surfers knew that simply attempting to "catch" these monsters meant dancing with extreme danger and possible death.

And so for decades the untamed waves rolled in, until technology and creativity inspired a man-made solution called "tow-in surfing." It requires a Jet Ski, which is fast and maneuverable enough to launch the surfers into these waves while assuring the safety of the driver. To see something as small as a surfer taming these giants is a testament to our resourcefulness and our urge to conquer challenges in the face of adversity.

We in the business community today find ourselves in a conundrum similar to that of these extreme surfers. Our "oceans" are changing, and the waves are growing bigger and more challenging to ride. Powerful forces in our markets are profoundly altering the landscape in which we compete as marketers and leaders. They are combining in a way that will either yield incredible creative energy or sink shareholder value.

These forces include: the rise of consumer connectivity via social media and the Internet; the fragmentation of media; and limits to growth imposed by severe cost cutting, which has supplanted our core purpose of providing our customers differentiated and compelling products and services.

How organizations respond to these forces and how they leverage a fourth—the incredible wealth of enabling technologies—will define those that survive and thrive. Those companies that fail to respond risk being crushed beneath the enormous waves of change we're experiencing now.

For instance, this fourth force of enabling technologies—and the consumer data they yield—requires that marketers continuously increase their investments in computing power, targeting tools, predictive models, and expert statisticians. These resources certainly expand what is possible for marketers in terms of understanding and communicating with customers, but that also means we must be ever more vigilant about what is reasonable when it comes to using the consumer's personal information.

There are no hard and fast rules for earning the right to use personal data, and marketers are navigating uncharted waters. The lesson is that data is a critical business asset for understanding what motivates specific purchasing decisions, but it could become a critical liability if mismanaged.

And so, in effect, these converging forces are producing perfect waves, but ones that are so large and powerful that without a proper strategy they pose a dire risk to many companies. The challenge for business leaders and marketers today is harnessing the power of all these forces, capturing the energy of the wave to carry their business forward, and placing the customer at the center of their purpose. The fundamentals of good branding and product development remain basically the same, but our role as marketers has been forever altered. Marketers are focusing intently on the customer, but these remarkable environmental shifts require companywide, systemic change that reaches far beyond brand and communications to include every touch point of the customer experience.

A few successful companies have embraced this transformation and can be found on various Top 100 lists, but customer management is no longer the purview of direct marketers or customer data strongholds like banks and retailers. You know the world has changed when traditional fast-moving consumer goods marketers and international beer barons preach "customer centricity"! Alexis Nasard of Heineken is a leading brand manager but in 2010 defined his company goals in customer terms: to develop "an everyday conversation with our customers."[1] José Parés, chief sales and marketing officer of Grupo Modelo (whose largest brand is Corona), also signed up for a data-driven strategy "focused on the specific demands" of its customers.[2] Can organizations ride this new consumer-controlled economy and arrive at a level of service best described as "intimate"?

Our ability to recognize these emerging waves and then use technology judiciously to capture their potential can propel us and help us create new experiences—and fuel the growth of our enterprises as a result. How we navigate these challenges will define which customers we keep and how we serve them.

Four Forces Conspire to Create the Perfect Wave

Today's organizations are at the center of an unprecedented period of transformation. But it is the very unparalleled nature of these events that provides us with a rich opportunity to step forward and demonstrate leadership in the face of change.

While we will deal with each force in turn, it is important to note they are interrelated, and together their scale is huge. Each force is the culmination of trends that have been moving independently for over a decade, but the way they are now combining in the market is what makes this script so compelling. Concerns about privacy are adding to the confluence of these four forces, creating a powerful undercurrent that makes the waters even more treacherous for marketers. The interactions among these four forces and privacy, and how we choose to deal with them, could very well define the winners and losers in the market.

The four forces are:

- the rise and fall of the CFO
- the fragmentation of media and the challenge of the attention economy
- consumer to the power of ten
- the capability revolution

Clearly each of these phenomena on its own is a meaningful challenge for any organization to contemplate, but we might also

be heading for a "cosmic car crash."[3] The maturation and convergence of all these movements will effect sweeping changes in the way companies and their customers interact. These shifts are providing a platform from which visionary organizations and leaders can reexamine the authenticity of their purpose. Will they place the consumer at the heart of their business efforts or continue to treat them as innocent bystanders in the race for results and shareholder value?

Before we explore these historic events at strategic levels, we should examine the four forces and fully underscore their impacts.

The Rise and Fall of the CFO

Managing the cost side of the ledger has always been an effective way to drive profit and shareholder value, and for many organizations it has turned into a crusade. Tremendous power has developed over the past two decades in those areas of the organization that are tasked with creating operational efficiency and expense reductions. This focus on efficiency and cost cutting has yielded strong results for companies. In fact, at most companies the rise of the Internet did more to drive shareholder value, via the increased efficiency of operations, than did the creation of new revenue streams.

The problem is that cost-based management can only take a company so far, and companies are beginning to recognize the limitations of the CFO mind-set. It is mathematically impossible for every organization to enjoy a cost advantage if its competitors are approaching the problem in the same way. In addition, most of the cost initiatives available to organizations have been implemented over the same period. Digitization, automation, offshoring, supply-chain management, downsizing, and the use of enterprise management software are all on the C-suite hit parade. Today's employee is working harder and more efficiently than the average employee of ten years ago, while the pace of innovation and change has accelerated dramatically.

In their classic business book on competitive differentiation, *The Discipline of Market Leaders,* Michael Treacy and Fred Wiersema identified three basic strategies for driving long-term competitiveness: efficiency, innovation, and customer intimacy. Efficiency has been maximized as much as realistically possible in most organizations. Innovation is the lifeblood of the technology and manufacturing fields but it is extremely difficult to achieve and even harder to sustain in other industries. Today's reality is that most organizations, in order to achieve sustainable growth, must increasingly compete through customer intimacy.

The cost-cutting efficiency mind-set of the past twenty years has delivered on the promise of improved earnings and corporate profitability and, in most instances, a positive spike in shareholder value. However, few companies have turned these advantages into meaningful and sustainable long-term growth. What I see in my peers in the Young Presidents' Organization, an association of roughly eighteen thousand business leaders from more than one hundred countries, is an urgent need for colleagues in their organizations to think about differentiating themselves competitively in this environment of change. Today's leaders are being pressed hard by the question: "How do I create profitable growth?"

The Fragmentation of Media and the Challenge of the Attention Economy

Switching gears, moving from companies to customers, we arrive at another principal transformation in today's business climate: the ongoing fragmentation of media; Internet-induced "power browsing"; and the ensuing attention scarcity among consumers.[4] [5]

To understand how media consumption has changed, just spend one day with any sixteen-year-old. Tomorrow's generation of customers has an incredible capacity to stream media in all its forms and across multiple channels of delivery. They appear to be doing their homework while watching television, surfing the Web, monitoring their Facebook accounts, and texting. But studies show they are not actually doing all of these things at the same time; they are rapidly moving from one to the other consecutively and losing time in between, making them less efficient than believed.[6] Altogether today's youth spend seven and a half hours a day on these combined media, according to a 2010 study by the Kaiser Family

Foundation.[7] That compares with six and a half hours a day five years before. But because they are multitasking they are actually consuming eleven hours of media in that seven-and-a-half-hour period. Yet while their ability to multitask may appear superior to that of the previous generation, the reality is that because of their consecutive movement from task to task, they are selectively tuning out everything except what is most important to them. Reaching these young consumers—capturing their attention and informing them of your products and services—is becoming an increasingly complex and difficult challenge.

The data broadly supports these assertions. Again, if we look at actual hours of media consumption we can see that the average consumer is racking up almost twice as much screen time today as he or she did just five years ago. And the adoption of gaming, the Internet, and cell phone technology means that it's consumed across twice as many channels.

Even the experience of television itself has changed dramatically. The proliferation of channels and specialty television has created more selective markets to target but at the same time increased the complexity of doing so. With the exception of a few major television programs, such as major sporting events or a highly successful series, reaching a broad consumer group is exceptionally challenging. Then factor in channel fragmentation with "time-shift TV," or the ability to download programming, or watch on demand, and engaging the consumer is akin to securing the proverbial brass ring.

The same challenges apply to other media, such as newspapers and magazines, as tablet devices like the Apple iPad proliferate.

Consumers are not immune to our efforts to get products in front of them, but they are only half listening. Arguably, there is no longer such a thing as the average consumer, but despite the explosion of segmented media and data targeting, our customers still face five thousand to ten thousand brand messages every day. Self-preservation dictates that they block out most of them, and only the relevant or the obnoxious break through. Consumers will pay greater attention to those messages that strike a resonant chord due to meaningful content, or a preexisting relationship with the brand.

Let's explore this notion of relationships for a moment. If Professor Robin Dunbar of Oxford University is correct and the human brain can only manage 150 relationships (Dunbar's Number), how do we get on the guest list?[8] Experience tells us that consumers take notice because they identify with the brand's attributes ("Just do it," of Nike, stain-fighting Tide, or the cachet of BMW), or it timely addresses a problem (buying a new car, funding retirement), or simply because they have a relationship with the brand.

The real challenge is that, thanks to the CFO mind-set, marketing budgets have not expanded proportionately to cover the increased ground established by the fragmentation and expansion of media opportunities. The net result is that marketers must be selective about which channels are best for their existing budgets. This in turn means that most marketers are jumping from channel to channel, either creating insufficient weight to be effective or taking their best guess—by choosing to focus their attention in only one area—thereby potentially missing a substantial portion of the consumer's attention economy. The easiest way to sum this up is with a mathematical equation:

Increasing fragmentation + decreasing consumer engagement + tighter budgets + more activity in more channels + greater scrutiny from the CFO = One BIG marketing problem.

Consumer to the Power of Ten

Word of mouth has always been a powerful force in marketing, and the rise of the Internet has increased this power exponentially. Anyone can blog or tweet their product preferences, or "like" a favorite brand on Facebook, and consumers are more likely to take the recommendation of a recognized or seemingly known person before believing what information they receive directly from a brand. Staying on top of all of these brand conversations has become the latest challenge for companies, and it will also become one of the most important tools for managing risks to their brands.

The Toronto International Film Festival is one of the largest film gatherings in the world. Each September people come from across the globe to promote their films, relying on the savvy film audience to give them the endorsements that lead to box office success. Prior to the festival in 2010, someone tweeted that they had been bitten by bedbugs at one of the primary theaters used for screenings. This set off a massive news response and public relations effort by the festival to mitigate the risk of bad attendance.[9] The claim was proven to be false; however, the incident illuminated the hazards brands face when consumers have a ready means of reaching out to the world.

Remember the public relations upheaval when a few consumers alleged that a new Pampers product gave their babies severe diaper rash? A Facebook group called "Pampers bring back the Old CRUISERS/SWADDLERS" grew to include more than ten thousand members, though the maker of Pampers, Procter & Gamble, maintained that it had received only two consumer complaints. According to branding expert Robert Passikoff, president of Brand Keys, "It doesn't matter if it's true or false; perception is everything."[10]

Another celebrated example involved the musician who put out a YouTube video called "United Breaks Guitars." Dave Carroll, the songwriter for the band Sons of Maxwell, says he witnessed United Airlines's baggage handlers abusing and breaking his thirty-five-hundred-dollar custom-made guitar, and that his repeated attempts to get United to take responsibility failed. Frustrated, he wrote and posted a song about the incident on YouTube. His campaign got United's attention, and the company made things right, but not before more than eleven million people had watched the protest video.[11]

What's happened in the last ten years has truly been exceptional. The entire relationship between a brand and its customers used to be a monologue. The brand decided what it stood for or what problem it solved and then broadcast that scripted message to consumers to inform them of the brand promise. If the product didn't live up to expectations, then consumers would attempt to get redress by asking to speak to the manager, writing a letter of complaint that was rarely answered to their satisfaction, or simply returning the product and taking their business elsewhere. Along the way, they'd tell their friends about it. None of these avenues got them very far, but they weren't looking for a relationship, just a refund.

The Web and e-mail became the dominant consumer channels, and the monologue became a dialogue. Using databases, call centers, and, most recently, the Internet as facilitating technologies, the company-customer link was made. But while that resulted in a more relevant and meaningful exchange between the parties, consumers still had limited options to voice and broadcast their concerns beyond attempting to start a viral e-mail campaign, or perhaps posting a blog. However, the balance of power was shifting, and it was the customers who forced the channels onto companies: "I'm on the Web. . . . You better come too if you want to find me."

Marketers recognized the commercial possibilities and made huge investments in customer relationship management (CRM) systems in the 1990s with the express purpose of building two-way relationships. But make no mistake: CRM was a customer-led revolution, and companies are still catching up.

Then social media came along, and this changed the game completely. There is now a "trialogue" in which the relationships are customer-to-community-members, and the company plays a voyeuristic role, just observing those interactions unless it has been invited into the conversation. This time the invitation said: "I'm on the Web with my friends. . . . You better come if you want to find us."

The explosion of online communities made the interaction event more like a block party or a rave. Customers are saying (to nobody in particular): "I'm on the Web with total strangers, but they also happen to love U2. That's all we have in common. . . . Figure out how to talk to us."

So now the power has shifted, and companies stand a very good chance of being uninvited, or "unsubscribed," from their most meaningful relationships. Today's brands need to find their voices and operate at a higher standard, and while social media can be a powerful tool for creating positive momentum around a successful product, it can just as quickly become a destructive force. Brands today are at greater risk than ever of being tried in the court of public opinion. This means that companies must ensure they create true brand advocacy, and ensure the authenticity of their efforts and claims.

The Capability Revolution

But achieving this level of legitimacy and, finally, intimacy in an increasingly savvy consumer mind is becoming proportionately more difficult as the channels and voices multiply. It requires a brain fine-tuned to both the potential and the current capabilities of measured marketing. This measured-marketing brain can conceive of greater complexity in its customer-management efforts and accomplish one-to-one communications on a mass scale. But while the technological advancements necessary to carry out these marketing programs have been made, the companies have not kept up organizationally. Ironically, their abilities to deepen customer relationships are still limited by their own relationships and the human factor.

First let's consider our technological accomplishments. The migration from the stages of one-to-many to one-to-few to one-to-one owes as much to databases and analytical tools as it does to the emergence of the Internet and digital media. The databases are bigger not only because of our ability to add more customers to our files, but also because in an effort to better segment and customize our offers we now track a lot more data on each individual. The typical grocery file can include thousands of data attributes per customer based on who the customer is, where he or she shops, and what offers he or she takes advantage of. And that's before you add scored variables from various predictive models.

The result is that databases are much more complex, often running into terabytes, and even, as is the case with eBay, petabytes. A decade ago this volume of data would have brought a simple analytical query to its knees, but our knowledge has also kept pace, and now we can structure these monsters to be so easily analyzed that we can nimbly extract the information necessary for the organization in minutes. Today's systems make it possible for analysts to sift through massive data sets quickly, in real time, and fully understand the behavioral intricacies of their customers.

Once the organization has segmented its customer base and established a responsible strategy for capturing that consumer's interest and encouraging her behavior, then the hard work begins. For many years this was where the system fell apart. Many great insights were simply too complex to be executed. Marketers, for example, could envision highly customized print mailings that offered consumers exactly what they wanted in a variety of product and service categories. Unfortunately, the limitations of plate printing made these visionary but complicated tactics impossible, because every customized element would require plate changes, and these were too costly and too complex to even contemplate. This all began to change thanks to the evolution of digital printing technology, which made customized printing both easier and dramatically more cost-efficient. Today's quantitative marketer has a wealth of options to help her achieve a one-to-one universe.

The digital domain in fact provides the perfect hothouse for the marketing community, and while we need to operate on a multichannel platform, the insular nature of the Web environment allows for near instant reaction time. Consumer data, conversations, and behaviors are all captured through click-stream data. That data is analyzed, customers are segmented into buckets of similar characteristics, individualized offers are created from a pool of preapproved messages, and real-time interactions occur without any traditional campaign planning. Of course, the quality of the interaction is correlated with the quality of the data provided by the consumer, but this is where customers become apprehensive, and justifiably so. It is unfortunate that data collecting is sometimes made to seem villainous when it is designed to enhance the relationship between shoppers and the companies with which they do business. The responsibility falls to marketers to ensure privacy at every step.

Digital data collection on the Web or through e-mail dramatically improves accuracy, delivery costs, and turnaround. It also gives the marketer a dynamic opportunity for relationship building through the sign-up process. Prospects are offered a choice of delivery options, additional content, language preferences, or the ability to share with a friend. Hence data collection becomes an engagement device. Additionally, variable content and dynamic offers can be triggered in real time. The end result is that the company and the customer can go from conversation to courtship in less time than it would have taken a bank manager in a past life to sign your account application in triplicate.

And now this same approach to marketing via e-mail and browsing can be taken on the road. Mobile marketing, where cellular phones and smartphones act as delivery channels, introduces location-based targeting as a dimension for customization. As the mobile technology improves, so will the level of marketing specificity. We are already moving from one-way text messaging to location-based applications that enable customers to receive local store offers, selected for them on the basis of their past behavior and present location, while they're pulling into the parking lot. The human capacity to grasp how we can leverage these technologies is running in tandem with what they can support effectively. But we are challenged with humanizing the analytics and adopting the organizational and cultural requirements to use these technologies in a way that makes sense to consumers. If the last two decades have proved anything, it is that a capability revolution is possible, and in many ways constant, especially in how it tasks us as organizations. Take into account the fact that 30 percent of four thousand executives said the biggest challenge inhibiting their use of analytics is that they don't understand how to use the data, according to a survey by the IBM Institute for Business Value and *MIT Sloan Management Review.* Meanwhile, only a third of the respondents had access to the information and analytics needed to do their jobs successfully.[12]

Our ability to create a full one-to-one experience is still in its infancy. While many organizations have embraced these technologies, a greater number continue on without a customer-specific view and without taking full advantage of the customer information they possess. That may prove to be the eventual downfall of many a great enterprise in today's enabled one-to-one economy, since this revolution shows no signs of slowing down.

Marketing Is the Next Frontier for Growth

Around the turn of the twentieth century the birth of consumer brands created a way for companies to differentiate their products, creating the revolution we know today as brand marketing. For more than eighty years, companies fine-tuned this marketing engine, first after the advent of radio and then of television. Up until the last decade most marketing was basically a variant of what appeared on these traditional channels and was based on the Four Ps—product, price, place, and promotion. Yet while there was evolution in the discipline of marketing and a boom in technology and channel and data applications, customer experiences have not changed fundamentally. If anything, they have become more mechanistic and overwhelming, as the media messages multiply.

Then everything shifted, seismically. While the Internet and digital marketing might not have altered the what, they did dramatically move the how.

If we believe that companies will not be able to continue to use cost cutting as their key to profitability, then we are on the cusp of a new era—an era in which marketers can reclaim their influence throughout the organization. Companies will once again have to invest in product innovation, and marketers will need to lead experience innovation. It goes back to the old adage: "The right product, to the right customer, at the right time" but conveyed in a manner that is meaningful and rewarding. It's a tall order. Marketing innovation will require the confluence of technology, data, media, capability, and relationships. The only sustainable way to do this is to intimately understand the customer and to meet the challenges presented by the fragmentation of the media and the customer's new powerful filters.

CHAPTER 2

Privacy: Are We Really Going to $%@# This Up?

In 1996, *Vancouver Sun* readers were treated to a full-page editorial about the AIR MILES program. The tone was decidedly alarmist:

> Writers of science fiction and thrillers have long fantasized about "Big Brother" agencies watching and controlling people's lives. What we are witnessing today is the birth of these "Big Brothers" in executive suites around the world.

The item went on to chronicle a frightening representation of how consumers' privacy was being violated by the AIR MILES data-collection machine.

> As the clerk slides [your] card through the reader, every detail of your purchase is added to an electronic profile owned by

> Loyalty Management Canada.* Your profile. It includes your name, gender, household size, annual income and date of birth. It has a record of the stereo you bought last October, the building materials you bought in the spring, your favorite brand of condoms, your deodorant and every other transaction you have logged on your Air Miles.[1]

And if the text wasn't worrisome enough, the *Sun* illustrated the piece with an illustration inspired by the classic sci-fi *War of the Worlds*, with the "eye" of the invading space ships replaced with the AIR MILES logo.

I'm probably not doing myself or my company any favors by giving the article added attention, but having been one of the leaders on the firing line, I was in a unique vantage point from which to examine the privacy question. The piece, with its falsehoods, captured the very worst fears about the collection and abuse of customer data. Few consumers have direct knowledge about where data goes and how it is managed, but they have a general sense of suspicion that can easily be whipped into paranoia. In the case of AIR MILES we were *not* collecting data at the level described and could not have linked condoms to stereos or to gender or anything else. More amazingly, whether through apathy, disbelief, or low readership, we thankfully received virtually no consumer complaints after the item appeared. Still, that doesn't let my company, or yours, off the hook.

As data-collection capability increases and marketers have become more creative about using consumer information, the practices of companies such as Netflix, Google, Facebook, and many

* Loyalty Management Canada became LoyaltyOne in 2008.

more have made headlines in traditional and social media. Privacy advocates and some consumers are expressing serious concerns about how marketers handle consumer data. The regulatory hounds are sniffing, and some are calling for strict legislation to control our industry.

The specter of Big Brother watching over consumers feeds a core myth in the marketing industry: Worries about privacy are making measured marketing an impossible dream for marketers, and privacy advocates have set out to hamstring innovation in customer management. Not to diminish the importance of customer advocacy, but the reality is that for most successful database marketers, a huge strategic advantage is gained from brokered data solutions that deliver value to both the business and the customer. Most privacy concerns are a product of a vocal, focused, well-organized, and well-intentioned minority, while the silent majority willingly shares its information with corporations that use the data responsibly and with the intent of creating mutual value.

The myth is driven by a lack of understanding, explosive journalism, and, in some cases, a lack of transparency and a failure to respect the individual's basic expectations of privacy and security. The privacy discussion invites factionalism, and it is easy to see how multinational corporations and the big online players have been cast in a sinister light. By separating fact from fiction we open up new avenues on which to drive marketing innovation and relationship building.

The Gold Rush, in Petabytes

As we've discussed, the capability revolution is in full swing, and technology is making data collection and analysis easier than it has ever been. Companies now have access to staggering amounts of data, and astonishing computing power. As of late 2010 Walmart was handling more than one million transactions every hour and feeding a database of more than 2.5 petabytes, the equivalent of 167 times the size of the books in America's Library of Congress. At the same time, Facebook housed forty billion photos.[2] By the time you sit down to read this book those numbers will surely have multiplied again. This massive processing and storage capacity is made possible by extraordinary computing power. Imagine: When researchers first set out to decode the human genome—a Herculean task that involved analyzing three billion base pairs—it took seven years. The same task could be accomplished in one week with today's computers.

Like the findings of the nineteenth-century California Gold Rush, data has become the raw material of business, and those companies that can mine it most effectively will make their fortunes. Craig Mundie, head of research and strategy at Microsoft, said, "What we are seeing is the ability to have economies form around the data—and that to me is the big change at a societal level, and even a macroeconomic level." On a more practical note, consider this question from Rollin Ford, the chief information officer of Walmart: "Every day I wake up and ask, 'How can I flow data better, manage data better, analyze data better?'"[3]

Cyanide, Mercury, and Data Leaks

We marketers are not always thinking clearly about the downstream impact on the consumer in our tremendous excitement around the flood of data, our rush to collect and mine it, and its potential for fueling new growth and innovation. In gold mining the continued exploration for new reserves has spawned extraction techniques using cyanide and mercury, which can be highly toxic to workers and the environment.[4]

Similarly, some of our industry's data practices are reckless and are feeding consumers' worries about privacy. We run the risk of salting our own game by reinforcing the belief that marketers are up to no good when we fail to balance customer interests against corporate pursuits. An array of bad practices is fueling consumer worries about data mining and privacy, and efforts toward establishing privacy laws are under way across the globe. According to the 2011 International Report, an annual publication by Privacy Laws & Business, a provider of privacy laws information, comprehensive privacy laws in the private sector now exist "in 76 jurisdictions around the world, and there are a few laws in the pipeline. The U.S. is not included here simply because it has no comprehensive Federal privacy law for the private sector."[5]

The outstanding and debatable question is whether enforced regulations really solve the problem. I suggest that some of the best methods for honest data use are those that are self-created. The U.S. business community has, for instance, taken proactive steps to self-regulate through the Advertising Option Icon, a blue logo that started appearing in the corners of online advertisements in 2011. When the consumer clicks on the icon a message appears stating that the ad "may have been matched to your interests based on your browsing activities," which means the ad is using behavioral targeting. The consumer then may choose to opt out from being tracked.[6] The icon, attached to roughly five billion ads, is part of a broader program by the Direct Marketing Association and is paid for entirely by businesses.[7]

This initiative is a good example of self-policing and responsible marketing. What else could we do better?

Data, Data Everywhere and Not a Plan in Sight

The logical starting point is in the data-collection process—when companies ask for data and then don't seem to do anything with it. When companies collect data and churn models in the background but continue to treat their customers with a one-size-fits-all approach, those customers become either annoyed or suspicious. We've all had experiences that make us question exactly why a company is collecting our personal information. Don't you hate it when the checkout person in a store asks for your phone number, e-mail address, or zip code without offering any explanation for why he or she wants it? What about retailers with a "membership" card for you to present at checkout that is clearly capturing data about your purchase but isn't linked to any program that rewards you with coupons or special offers in return? Once in a while you may get a mailing or a discount on your purchase, but the accumulation system is so shrouded in mystery that you never know when to expect the next message. This hideaway strategy is low risk to the company and low return to the consumer, but beyond being an inadequate marketing effort, it makes consumers uncomfortable. If you're not using this data to create better offers for me, what exactly are you doing with it?

But data collection for no clear purpose is more than annoying; it can be frightening for consumers. In 2010, Google came under international fire for collecting personal information, including e-mails, from unprotected Wi-Fi networks through its Street View cameras. The company was sued in several U.S. states,[8] while in Canada the privacy commissioner ruled that Google had committed a "serious violation of Canadians' privacy rights."[9] In Germany, where Google faced spirited protests by German officials, it eventually opted out of expanding Street View, despite a ruling by the Berlin State Supreme Court that Street View was legal.[10]

Google said the data collection was an unintentional result of a programming error, and that it was destroying the data. But many people were not comforted by those assurances (more than 244,000 Germans had opted out of Street View by April 2011).[11] More to the point, regardless of whether data collection is intentional or unintentional, the more salient issue regards the collection of personal data for no clearly defined purpose. This is precisely the kind of event that worries privacy advocates. When a company searches for personal information without clearly communicating its intention it damages the reputation of all organizations that collect and use customer data. When one of us slips up—especially a large player like Google—the entire industry suffers the consequences of the bad public relations it causes.

Some companies like to ask for data, creating the expectation that they will use it to provide you with something special, but then ignore what you've told them. This is a clear case of hedging your bets. You ask the customer for his or her preferences, but if those characteristics do not fit the predefined experience you've designed, then you opt for the mass approach and ditch the customer file. Think of the hotel loyalty program that asks in great detail about a guest's preferences. She dutifully completes the survey, specifying a high floor away from the elevator and a soft pillow, preferably poly-filled because of her sensitive allergies. This is a good customer who appreciates that the hotel cares enough to customize her future experiences. The next time she checks in during convention season, however, she finds herself in a room on the second floor across from the elevator, with a pillow so firm it hurts her neck.

With data comes accountability. Businesses asking for data establish expectations in the minds of their customers; if they do not use it responsibly they have failed to deliver on those expectations. This practice does more harm than good, and a company would be better off not asking at all than bypassing the stated preferences. What's worse, companies are more likely to engage their high-spend, high-frequency customers in this futile data-collection exercise, so the cost of their failed attempt at data management can cost them their best customers.

The Bottomless Data Pit

The explosion in the availability of data, plus the capacity to manipulate it, has created a kind of virtual cookie jar for marketers—and the temptation to keep reaching in for more and more. And therein lies the risk: How many times can we dip in before we've gone too far in compromising customer privacy? Clearly our eyes can be bigger than our stomachs. Who decides how far is too far? Is there a simple mechanism to keep data greed in check?

I recently had the opportunity to sit down with a number of privacy officials, and as we talked about data and privacy and the risks developing in the marketplace, the cookie jar metaphor came back to life. Just as kids can't control their impulses to keep reaching in, many marketers have trouble managing the urge to collect more than the necessary amount of data. This struggle to balance need against real capabilities—call it a lack of frontal cortex control—is the reason why privacy advocates, regulators, and privacy commissioners are created to protect consumer interests.

What We Should Have Learned from Direct Marketing

Many of the challenges facing database marketers today are unmistakably similar to those faced by direct-mail marketers and telemarketers, and today's measured marketers would do well to heed the valuable lessons to be learned from these industries.

There have long been efforts to strike a balance between the individual's right to control his or her personal information and privacy with an organization's ability to collect and use that data for business purposes. Companies have historically taken the broadest interpretation of regulations on what data they can keep, how they acquire that data, what systems they can use to connect that data, and the necessity of asking the consumer explicitly to opt in or out. On the other hand, governments, regulators, and commissioners have tended to want to impose greater control, sometimes in response to real or imagined threats voiced by consumer and advocacy groups. The critical issues have been protection of privacy, integrity in the system, and the ability of the consumer to choose not to participate.

The direct-mail and telemarketing industries gambled on the loosest possible application of regulatory restrictions on their activities. Today online marketers are taking exactly the same tack, bending the rules and, in some cases, disregarding them. Internet marketers have operated beyond the norms established by the traditional direct-marketing industry for two reasons: First, they are able to track and target the consumer differently in this new environment; and second, the traditional rules were not built expressly for the digital age.

But it can be very risky bypassing the basic principles learned over the decades during which the direct-mail and telemarketing companies interacted with consumers. The aggressive activities of telemarketers eventually led to legislation that hobbled the entire industry with the advent of do-not-call lists. Online marketers are at a crossroads now, facing the very real possibility of legislative regulation that would severely curb our activities. Can we learn from the example of telemarketing and regulate our own activities, easing the concerns of consumers and privacy advocates?

Privacy: What's the Fuss About?

Let's face it: Privacy has been a concern for consumers since records were first kept. Some information has always been publicly available. In the United States, some personal political donations and the price of your house are all matters of public record. But prior to the advent of the Internet, it took some effort to track down that information. The Internet and system integration have fundamentally changed our relationship with information, both in terms of the ease of collecting it and the hazard of having our cross-enterprise, multichannel activities exposed. I love this quote by Lee Tien, a senior staff attorney at the Electronic Frontier Foundation, who says that, prior to the Internet, "you were private by default and public by effort. Nowadays, you're public by default and private by effort."[12]

While it may be folklore that privacy concerns render database marketing impossible, it's no myth that consumers are concerned about privacy. They practice a spectrum of protective actions that ranges from deleting cookies to using cash for all transactions, yet at the same time, legitimate debates are arising among companies, consumers, privacy advocates, and regulatory bodies.

That's Kind of Creepy

First, at a purely gut level it just feels creepy when consumers realize that companies are able to identify their individual behavior, both online and in the stores they visit. Although intuitively they understand that search-engine marketing gives them recommendations based on past Web activity, it is jarring when they have an incongruent experience. Consumers are jolted out of their contented state and, like walking behind the screen in a puppet show, they become conscious of the mechanics behind the experience and react negatively.

Tracking feels like an invasion of privacy, and justifiably so. Uncertainty about what's being monitored and how the information is being used raises the creepy quotient. Media reports about companies that misuse customer data or about sneaky online data-collection practices do nothing to allay the fears of consumers who are already on high alert that their trust might be being violated.

There's no doubt that there are some disturbing practices out there. A friend recently told me that when he arrived in his room at a major luxury hotel he found a Coke and a Mars bar waiting for him in his welcome packet. He thought it was odd until he remembered that the last time he had stayed at that hotel he had wolfed down a snack of a Coke and a Mars bar before heading to the airport. Apparently, whoever cleaned his room after he checked out went through his waste bin and made a note of his eating habits, and the hotel's welcome program duly noted his preferences. I think we can agree that's going too far, and that if a hotel chain wants to know what you'd like in your welcome packet, it would do better to ask you rather than to engage in Dumpster diving. Such inept data practices can easily go from the disturbing to the distressing. In 2010, Facebook was implicated in an advertising scheme that enabled it to target gays and lesbians using a unique identifier, including the IP address.[13]

Creating satisfying experiences using consumer data can be a windfall for your customers, but your most brilliant innovation should always be checked for incongruence.

But Who Told You That You Could Do That?

Beyond the creepy factor, consumers have legitimate concerns about their individual rights and expectations when it comes to data collection and use. Specifically, consumers feel they should have the right to choose whether or not their data is shared, the right to choose what types of data can be tracked and shared, and the right to know what's being done with that data. A 2010 study by Forrester Research confirmed that many consumers are uncomfortable handing over control of their data to other parties. In response to a statement, 91 percent of respondents agreed that they would prefer to retain control of their own data. However, a portion of those same customers also indicated that either the government or companies could also participate in that control process.[14] This clearly demonstrates a level of market confusion about who should play the primary role.

What exactly are consumers concerned about? Our own 2011 survey of two thousand American and Canadian consumers shows: 81 percent of respondents fear companies commonly share their personal information without the consumer's permission; 85 percent said they are often concerned about how much of their personal information is being held by others; 76 percent are worried that their behavior is being tracked while they are online; and one third said they have been notified that their personal information has been compromised.[15]

Underscoring our own findings is a study by the Poneman Institute, which asked nearly seven thousand respondents to rank their greatest worries about privacy on the Web.[16] Not surprisingly, identity theft ranked first, with 59 percent of respondents indicating it as the most serious privacy-related threat.

In an environment where data collection and sharing is not managed with transparency, you leave it to the potentially dangerous imagination of the consumer. Consumers worry that data tracking could: jeopardize their ability to get insurance; damage their credit; or expose deeply personal information, such as sexual orientation. As Tien points out, "There are all sorts of inferences that can be made about you from the websites you visit, what you buy, who you talk to. What if your employer had access to information about you that shows you have a particular kind of health condition or a woman is pregnant or thinking about it?"[17]

What's Going On Behind the Scenes?

Fears about violations of rights and expectations thrive in conditions where visibility is poor. Put simply, consumers feel they can't see what marketers are doing with their data behind the scenes, and they don't trust marketers to protect their data appropriately. In the Forrester study, 41 percent of respondents indicated that they did not trust anyone—neither businesses nor governments—with their data.

This lack of visibility also means that consumers cannot correct any errors in their personal data. By contrast, they have access to their credit reports and a clear means to correct any errors. In fact, if they subscribe to one of the many credit services out there, consumers can be alerted every time someone searches their data. Not so with data collected about their browsing and buying behaviors. A major concern of privacy advocates is lack of full visibility, that consumers not only don't know what is being said about them, but also that they have not given explicit permission to companies to share and act on it. We have operated AIR MILES from the beginning under the philosophy that we would not collect and use anyone's personal information unless we have been given clear permission by the consumers to do so.

In the spring of 2011 the music-streaming service Pandora was accused of sending "mass quantities" of personal data—including age, sex, zip code, and precise geographic location—from its mobile applications for the purpose of serving cell phone advertising. Pandora's Android application was found to integrate with five different cell phone advertisement libraries,[18] and all without the knowledge or consent of users. When this kind of activity happens behind the scenes, consumers feel powerless.

Now You're Really Annoying Me

An environment of low visibility naturally gives rise to speculation about what marketers might be doing with data. But consumers' concern about privacy isn't just speculative. Some data sharing and online tracking result in truly annoying outcomes for consumers. I'm sure we've all experienced those online ads that follow you wherever you go on the Web, opt-out boxes on Web pages that are obviously designed to be overlooked, and overfrequent e-mails from eager retailers. The online retailer Zappos.com was criticized for too frequent ads that in effect trailed consumers online like pushy salesmen. "We took that brick-and-mortar pet peeve and applied it online," said Darrin Shamo, Zappos.com's director of direct marketing. Consumers who shopped for lingerie on Zappos .com also complained that lingerie ads kept popping up when their kids were using the computer. Others complained that these persistent pop-up ads inadvertently revealed Christmas presents they had bought online to family members who shared the computer. Preserving online privacy is more complicated than Zappos.com—or any of us—initially anticipated.

Zappos.com has since adjusted its contact management approach and toned down its targeting. Ads are less frequent. In addition, the new ads are transparent about what Zappos.com knows about its consumers and where it obtained that information. The new approach also offers the consumer an opportunity to opt out of seeing the ads altogether. Zappos.com intends to test the new approach for response effectiveness, but it has stated that it is willing to get out of the business altogether if it can't get it right.[19] Zappos.com figures, quite rightly, that it's better to have a loyal customer and to touch that customer less frequently than to alienate its customers with annoying ads and e-mails.

Who's Looking Out for Me?

An obvious concern of consumers and privacy advocates alike is the safety of the data entrusted to companies. Yet it is a concern that companies still can't put to rest. Sony suffered a public relations disaster in early 2011 when a hacker compromised the data—including the credit card information—of seventy-seven million Sony PlayStation users. Sony cautioned in a letter to users:

> Although we are still investigating the details of this incident, we believe that an unauthorized person has obtained the fol-

> lowing information that you provided: name, address (city, state, zip), country, e-mail address, birth date, PlayStation Network/Qriocity password and login, and handle/PSN online ID. . . . While there is no evidence at this time that credit card data was taken, we cannot rule out the possibility. Out of an abundance of caution we are advising you that your credit card number (excluding security code) and expiration date may have been obtained.[20]

The first class-action lawsuit was filed the very next day.

But even the most state-of-the-art protective measures won't shield a consumer's personal information from straight-out abuse—such as using it for unstated reasons. Companies are obligated to protect the data they collect even from legitimate entities, including government officials. An example dear to my heart is the British grocery and general merchandise giant Tesco. The government twice requested to delve into its customer data and Tesco steadfastly resisted both times. In 2003, Tesco rebuffed calls from British members of Parliament to share data that would reveal purchasers of junk food and high-fat foods as part of a healthy-eating public relations campaign.[21] Then, in a move that one commentator described as "vaguely Orwellian," the British government once again approached Tesco when it was revamping the 2011 census, in an attempt to get it to share the data collected in its Clubcard program to help overhaul the nation's census.

In fact, Tesco was not alone. The British government approached a number of major banks, retailers, and utilities to gain access to their customer data. Tesco refused, and stuck firmly to its guns. According to Clubcard director Janet Smith, "One of the key reasons our customers trust Clubcard is because they know Tesco would never compromise on the promise we make them. There's no wriggle room, we just don't break that promise. To do so would be to jeopardize not only customers' trust, but also the success of the scheme."[22]

But What Do I Get Out of It?

A final perspective on data gathering and mining has to do with the value of consumer data and the equitable exchange of value for information. Consumers are increasingly aware that what's free on the Web isn't really free: The price they pay for access to the Web is the information they reveal about themselves through their behavior. When you surf Google you're sharing your interests. Google then commercializes this information, which is then packaged into advertising that targets you. This happens despite the fact that some consumers may actually prefer to be exposed to a wider variety of products or services.

Many consumers know, even on a subconscious level, that there is real value inherent in the information companies collect about them and have an implicit understanding of the value exchange that should be taking place. This value exchange should be more or less equitable in the ideal world. When companies make appropriate and responsible use of this data, consumers will experience its benefits and be more likely to want to participate. The proposition to the consumer is: Allow us to collect this data about your browsing and buying behaviors, and we'll provide you with offers that are valuable to you—discounts, attractive products, coupons, and other benefits. Consumers are becoming increasingly alert about whether they are receiving sufficient value in exchange for their information.

In few cases has the question of value been more public than in the ongoing controversy over privacy on Facebook. In 2010 and 2011, Facebook users repeatedly questioned if they were getting equal value for all the personal info they gave. Even the benign, feel-good activity of "liking" a company or brand led to unwitting endorsements by some of its members. It was revealed in early 2011 that Facebook was selling companies the lists of "likes" and similar activities of Facebook users, which were then parlayed into "sponsored stories"—paid ads that featured the user and were sent to that user's Facebook friends.[23]

When this feature was launched—quietly—Facebook did not include an option to decline inclusion in these word-of-mouth ads, and privacy advocates argued that Facebook was making money from its users' names without their consent. Making matters even less transparent, Facebook announced the strategy in a video on its marketing page, a page that few Facebook users were even aware of at the time.

By not posting news of its sponsored stories program on its blog or home page, where it would have received more attention, Facebook was behaving as if it had something to hide. Facebook's lack of prominent clarity, and the lack of an opt-out option, cost the company loyalty. This is a call for transparency, and a call to further nurture an environment in which companies are encouraged to ask for explicit permission.

The worst part for Facebook (and its subscribers) was that the sponsored stories incident followed by one year a class-action settlement involving its Beacon advertising system. Beacon, launched in 2007, published without their prior knowledge or consent what its members were buying and using on other Web sites. What's worse, through Beacon the company was tracking their Web shopping activity even after they had logged off the Facebook site. The backlash was immediate and intense. A $9.5 million settlement was reached in March 2010 on behalf of 3.6 million members. Facebook was ordered to earmark $6 million of that settlement toward a "digital trust fund": Organizations would receive grants to study online privacy. Facebook by then had already shut down the service.[24]

Lastly, in November 2011, two years after changing its privacy settings without asking its users' permission, Facebook agreed to a Federal Trade Commission order barring it from deceiving consumers. The settlement was followed by two weeks of news reports that Facebook was tracking the Web activity of its 800 million members, as well as nonmembers who happened to visit its site.[25] As part of the FTC order, Facebook was required to submit to twenty years of privacy audits. In a blog post, CEO Mark Zuckerberg insisted that Facebook has a good history of transparency but "I'm the first to admit that we've made a bunch of mistakes."[26]

What Consumers Want: Transparency and Relevance

Given all their worries about privacy, it's a wonder that consumers want to engage online at all. Fortunately they do, but they have some very clear conditions under which they join the party. The key issues from their point of view are transparency and relevance. Consumers want to know what we're doing with the data we collect and how it's going to benefit them. According to Fran Maier, executive director of TRUSTe, a major provider of Internet privacy services, "We have a solid indication that consumers want us to find a way to get them the advertising that is relevant to them. In order to do this, behavioral targeting is one of the most promising methods, but at the very least it has to be made more transparent, provide choices, and deliver real value."[27]

Unfortunately, not all companies have met these standards consistently: It was discovered in April 2011 that Apple had been using its iPhones and iPads as tracking devices, sensors that revealed users' whereabouts through nearby cell towers and Wi-Fi hot spots. In other words, iPhones and iPads were keeping track of all locations their owners visited, from the grocery to the car wash.

Apple was not alone in this practice; Google was also collecting customer location data. What was their perceived motivation? That such information not only improves the accuracy of maps and similar services, but it also enables marketers to design spot-on advertising messaging. In one *New York Times* story, the information was said to be so valuable that Apple and Google were described as "willing to push the envelope on privacy to collect it."[28] According to the business research and consulting firm Frost & Sullivan, the cell phone advertising market could reach $2.5 billion by 2015. Add location, and those spots become even more valuable.

Though some security analysts said they did not believe Apple was tracking individuals, lawmakers in the United States and Europe called for investigations and explanations.[29]Apple did not help itself: It waited a full week before responding to the allegations, through a Q&A on its Web site. There Apple said it did not track the precise location of iPhone users and had no plans to do so in the future. Rather, it said its data files consisted only of Wi-Fi hot spots and cell towers that surrounded iPhone users. That might have been enough to reassure die-hard Apple loyalists, but the company still allowed Big Brother–type headlines to dominate the press in the interim.

The lack of transparency in the Apple case highlights a key

concern for consumers: Most people realize that information is being tracked and they are okay with that; what they object to is that the occasional offer to opt in—if the option is presented at all—is often buried or mired in trickery. Do companies think these roadblocks secure customer relationships? That's like saying handcuffs ensure lawfulness. Likewise, the opt-out process should not require several steps and a user's manual. The rule of thumb, according to our sister company, Epsilon, which is one of the largest e-mail marketing services in the world, is to make the opt-out as easy as possible, preferably one or two clicks. According to a 2011 survey of retailers by Epsilon, 55.6 percent of respondents said they required two clicks, and 16 percent required just one. (One click, however, may limit the retailer's ability to reach the customer at other touch points and eliminate the consumer's ability to manage preferences such as e-mail frequency.)[30]

Experience shows us, though, that most customers are comfortable with data collection as long as it's transparent and provides benefits relevant to them. Amazon.com is perhaps the most frequently cited example of a business built on data stores and recommendation engines. It is best known for using the purchase histories of its returning customers as a means to recommend items and content that reflects their implied preferences, such as music in a genre previously purchased.

The early 1990s can rightfully be described as the Wild Wild West of database building. There were few controls, and firms didn't think twice about sending customer files via e-mail or storing them on hard drives under desks. When we launched AIR MILES in 1992 we were pioneers in data management. We were collecting and managing customer-transaction data, through our coalition-loyalty program, for more than one hundred companies, so from day one we held ourselves to a higher standard. Our database principles governed data collection, access, usage, frequency, and contact management. Through the years, as consumers engaged in the data conversation, we raised the bar to stay ahead of their growing expectations. The AIR MILES privacy policy is rigorously explicit regarding what we're collecting and why, and we make it very clear to consumers that they can opt out at any time. Consumers have control over whether they receive offers from us and how they receive them. More than ten million Canadian households are active in our program, with an opt-out rate of less than 0.01 percent. And while consumers in Canada have the legal right to request their data history from any company, we've had fewer than one hundred requests from customers to examine their data over the twenty years the program has been in operation. The AIR MILES program is clear proof that if you respect consumer expectations, create simple and transparent principles, and offer real value in exchange, the vast majority of customers will not only tolerate but actually embrace data-driven marketing.

Is There a Grand Reckoning Coming?

I like to think of customer innovation like water: a subterranean stream seeking an alternate path through the seams and cracks in the walls imposed by both the legal system and social norms.

Technology now allows us marketers to garner a disproportionate amount of very personal information and use it for targeting purposes. If you have a killer idea for customer innovation and an equity mind-set, this could be the start of something big. But if the idea is half formed, and along the way you are tempted to grab one more cookie from the jar to accumulate more data for a rainy day, think again. If customer marketers and online businesses are careless they risk the fate of telemarketers, who have been legislated to the point of ineffectiveness. At this moment we are on course for a grand reckoning: Either the industry will become accountable or legislation will hold it to account. Measured marketing carries amazing promise for both organizations and consumers alike. If we collect and use customer data responsibly, we not only improve shareholder value, but we can provide unimaginable benefits to our customers. There is a tremendous opportunity for all.

If the marketing industry can step up and behave responsibly, everyone will benefit. If not, it will be taken out of our hands, and we will never realize the potential for what might have been.

CHAPTER 3

Making the Leap: How Do I Achieve Growth Through Customer Intimacy?

Back in the mid 1990s, the Canadian marketplace was facing a gas crisis that had little to do with prices, fuel shortages, or taxes. Instead, this crisis involved locations, and it took a loyalty program to help fix it.

The market was overstored, meaning there were far too many stations operating along our roadways and a disproportionate number of them did not meet consumer expectations for greater convenience, pay at the pump, and ease of use. The industry was overdue for rationalization so that its many smaller, outdated locations were closed, relocated, or retrofitted into larger, more profitable self-service stations.

Enter our AIR MILES partner, Shell, which set a rather ambitious goal: It planned to reduce its network by 20 percent, from twenty-five hundred to roughly two thousand sites, while also renovating a significant number of its remaining stations to stay competitive.

Maintaining market and customer share while reducing locations is about as difficult for any retail organization as changing the wings on an airplane in midflight. But Shell was already well down the customer management path and had a secret weapon in its arsenal. It had access to customer information through its partnership with AIR MILES that represented a majority of its sales volume. Shell's challenge was to mine this data to accomplish three critical tasks:

- identify which Shell sites should be closed permanently and which had potential, but required a site renovation;
- transfer customers of those closed stations to nearby Shell locations, essentially retaining business and market share;
- ensure that the renovated gas stations, once reopened, quickly recaptured those relocated customers.

We helped Shell achieve this task by digging into the numbers to identify established shopping practices, define driving patterns, and design a marketing and awareness program to direct its consumers to new locations. We found, for instance, that members of the AIR MILES program accounted for more than half of each location's total revenue, and of those customers, 50 percent generated 86 percent of those sales. This was the target market. By understanding their behaviors, including their shopping patterns not only at Shell but also at the other merchants within our loyalty coalition, we could predict which sites these customers would turn to once their regular locations closed.

The approach was elegant in its simplicity and focus. First we alerted customers of a location's upcoming renovations through direct-mail and in-store marketing and guided them to the nearest (and most likely) alternate site. Then, as an incentive to stick with Shell during the shift, we offered them double AIR MILES for purchases made at that second station. After the renovation Shell provided a suite of welcome-back teasers, including direct mailers offering double and triple reward miles, and made a site-reopening announcement to encourage customers to come back to their newly improved and preferred location.

Of course, there were preexisting challenges. For one thing, fuel customers are highly likely to switch brands. Unlike dry cleaners or supermarkets, gas stations are often selected based on price and convenience. A move across the street could result in a dramatic sales shift.

Add to this the fact that a gas station renovation typically takes six weeks. If a customer fills up once a week, that translates to six occasions when he or she could choose a different brand. It was critical that we identify the right alternate station and motivate Shell's customers to change their behavior in the company's favor by making it their new destination as quickly as possible.

So what happened? As a result of good planning and effective data use, Shell was able to retain about 75 percent of its customer volume during the renovations, up from the industry standard of 25 percent. A very strong finish for Shell and our loyalty offers, but one we've seen repeatedly when using customer data and rewards to change behavior. In this case, careful attention to designing a desired customer experience delivered astonishing results. Shell's renovated stores were able to regain their former volume in half the projected time, and in response to offers, customers actually increased their overall spending by an average of 7 percent. Yes, you read that correctly. Shell closed a customer's most frequently used location, and that customer actually spent *more* at Shell during the renovation by driving *farther* to buy its gas.

How did Shell overdeliver on experience? It communicated openly with loyal customers, recognizing their brand affiliation and talking to them as Shell "insiders." It sent communications that openly acknowledged the inconvenience caused by the construction. And to help offset that disruption, it offered double or triple miles as an incentive to stick it out with Shell during the renovation.

Shell also evolved during this process from Canada's least efficient major fuel retailer (ranking fourth) to the most efficient, on the basis of volume per site, a position it still holds today. All this while maintaining market share in what could have been a major period of customer churn and dissatisfaction among its most loyal customers.

"The AIR MILES program provided a very, very effective tool for doing what we'd never had the means to do before," said Terry Plomske, Shell's manager of marketing communications at the time.

Customer Intimacy: ~~Knowing~~ Fixating on Customer Needs

It is this kind of deep connection with customers—understanding and anticipating their needs and going the extra mile to meet them—that is at the heart of customer intimacy. As I mentioned earlier, the phrase "customer intimacy" was originally coined by Treacy and Wiersema in the book *The Discipline of Market Leaders*.[1] They identified three value disciplines in it that have withstood the test of time to ensure profitable growth and success:

- **operational excellence**: efficiently providing the customer with a reliable product or service;
- **product leadership:** developing products that consistently redefine the state of the art; and
- **customer intimacy:** providing the customer with a total solution for his or her needs, not just a product or service.

Let's look at each discipline. In terms of operational excellence, Walmart is the gold standard, but really, any organization that puts an extreme focus on quality management, logistics, and its supply chain would qualify. The digital and tech sectors usually dominate in product leadership. Apple topped *Fast Company*'s 2011 World's Most Innovative Companies list, not just for its incredible product designs, but also for having platforms that spawned "an ecosystem of creativity, from gaming to finance to chip making."[2] Applying my own customer lens, I would give honorable mentions to Twitter, Cisco, Foursquare, Groupon, LinkedIn, and Amazon for designing products that transform the customer experience. And harkening back to my days at Quaker Oats, I'd give kudos to the packaged goods industry as a whole, and Kraft in particular, for its brilliant redefinition of the snack category when it invented the one-hundred-calorie packs for portion control.[3]

As for the third discipline, customer intimacy, it is in some respects the hardest to measure, because the ultimate arbiter of success is the consumer. Many companies proclaim that they focus on the customer and strive for shopper retention, but few are dedicated to managing an end-to-end customer journey and to fostering the emotional connection that defines genuine loyalty. The travel, hospitality, and specialty retail sectors usually have this category sewn up, but the up-and-comers are banks, insurance, and financial services firms that are competing for customer trust and engagement. American Express, Fidelity Investments, and Barclaycard are the brands that immediately spring to mind.

OK, but Where Does My Company Fit In?

Excelling in any one of these categories is not a simple undertaking. Two or three players set the standard for the industry, and all the others scramble for points of differentiation. With giants dominating the market, is there any hope for competitors? The answer is yes, and the formula exists within that enigmatic discipline of customer intimacy. Surprisingly, it is easier for business-to-business companies to focus on customer intimacy than it is for consumer-facing companies. If Hewlett-Packard, Microsoft, or IBM chooses to wrap its arms around its top one thousand customers, each has the account histories, the relationship sales teams, and the supporting service-enhancement technologies such as sales force automation tools to do so. Most important, each has a sizable margin-per-customer, enabling it to invest in personalizing the experience of every client.

Still, for most industries, the complexity of data segmentation, customer value analysis, and digitization have increased exponentially over the last twenty years. These tools have enabled companies to know their customers better than ever before and to design data-driven customized experiences at the segment and customer level. There is a wealth of opportunity in the data companies collect today for those that can't shave costs like Walmart or innovate as well as Apple, allowing them to create one-of-a-kind relationships with their customers that will extend customer life and their bottom line.

Are You an Imposter or the Real Thing?

Of course all companies have the requisite customer affirmations in their annual reports and on their Web sites, where they profess their undying love for customers and make lofty declarations that are too vague to be measurable. Those are not the companies of which I write. What distinguishes a customer-centric organization is exactly that: the customer is at its center. Product development starts with the customer's unmet needs; employee training starts with customer expectations; IT investment starts with customer requirements. Truly customer-intimate companies operate on a different plane. A customer-intimate company reaches beyond the simple execution of the business model—having the lowest prices or the fastest service—and shapes its strategies around the daily demands of its best customers. Sure, its shoppers may be price-sensitive or time-starved, but some of them may also be environmentally conscious, newly pregnant, or recently retired. Many just want to have a consistently pleasant experience and to be recognized.

Hello, Hello, Anybody Out There?

While Treacy and Wiersema paint clear dividing lines between each strategic model, the reality is that businesses may move from one model to the other, or be divided in their focus, as they evolve. With the rapid pace of expansion of the wireless industry, it is perhaps the best example of a category in transition. Wireless providers could trace their competitive dominance to product, packaging, and marketing innovation as the business grew dramatically in the last two decades, with a nod to operational efficiency in the building and management of network performance. The balance of innovation, however, has tipped more recently to the developers of operating systems, such as Apple and Android, handset manufacturers such as Samsung, Nokia, and Motorola, and every large- and small-scale application developer operating from its garage. So where will China Mobile, BT (British Telecom), Vodafone, AT&T, and Rogers Communications compete in the future? You can be sure they're focused on the customer experience, but it's not for the reasons you think. First and foremost, theirs will be an efficiency play, since the cost of servicing their customers is one of their largest balance sheet liabilities and operational headaches. Customer churn has always been their Achilles' heel from a marketing standpoint, and they have effectively managed retention through contracts and product introductions. But if innovation is no longer in their direct control, then what will be the next shiny object to attract customers?

Are Groceries a Product or an Experience?

Don't get me wrong. Firms organized around operational excellence or product leadership also want to fulfill the customer's needs—but not in a way that will sacrifice the business model.

Consider, for example, a supermarket. The traditional, product-centric approach to the grocery business requires that stores carry the brands and goods that drive maximum sales and profits. Retailers have relied for years on traditional supply-chain and category-management techniques to fulfill these operational goals. They measure their business performance using metrics such as sales per square foot, average basket size, and inventory turns. Rarely do you come across a grocery chain that thinks in terms of return on customer. Then Tesco emerged with shopper analytics, followed closely by the environmentally conscious Whole Foods, with its premium products, freshly prepared meals, and organic, gluten-free foodstuffs.[4] [5] Chains like Tesco and Whole Foods redefined the playbook with their focus on customers, data, and experience and thankfully, traditional grocers took up the customer charge.

Today's capabilities for customer insight and technology empowers retailers to compete in a different way, first by identifying the points of pain their customers experience when interacting with them, and then by reworking the store's design, inventory, or promotions to deliver the most favorable solution. The products and services themselves may change very little in a customer-intimate model, but simply building experiences around the ease of access and simplicity of use may be enough to start the repositioning exercise. Setting a keen eye to pricing and shopper analytics is the science behind customer bonding. And an added injection of empathy, trust, and transparency in their customer communications suddenly puts retailers in the business of building intimate relationships.

If there is any doubt that the customer-intimate model is a more appropriate approach for the supermarket industry, consider this statistic, by Win Weber: Of decisions made in the supermarket, 74 percent are made "off-list," or in the aisle.[6] This means that the bulk of incremental spending is actually motivated by the in-store experience.

And if there is any doubt that customer intimacy is an unmet need, consider this statistic from American Express and its Global Customer Service Barometer: Only 24 percent of customers believe companies go the extra mile for them, and 21 percent believe that companies take their business for granted.[7]

Customer-intimate companies put the customer at the center of their purpose and build their strategy from there, enacting Peter Drucker's famous edict: "There is only one valid definition of business purpose: to create a customer."[8]

Sounds Nice, but What About the Bottom Line?

But if the relationship between a company and its customer should be like that of good neighbors, where does the bottom line factor in? Is customer management too touchy-feely for the CFO? Is the notion of customer lifetime value and relationship building too lofty and imprecise for shareholders to rally behind? Naturally, every company has to keep an eye on business results and quarterly earnings.

Short-term profitability for customer-intimate companies is counterbalanced by the long-term value of their greatest assets: their customers. These companies measure a customer's worth not by a few transactions but over her lifetime, by multiplying the annual sales she is expected to generate by the number of years she is projected to shop with the company. Once the value equation is fine-tuned, so that future profits can be correlated with a customer's predicted lifetime spending, then customer relationships can be proven to contribute to company growth.

Predicted lift in revenue associated with a customer's behavioral change has always been the lifeblood of target marketing. For years direct marketers have rallied for their portion of the total ad budget on the basis of measured customer value and expected sales.

When the luxury automaker Audi set out to build its existing customer loyalty program, for instance, it knew that its customers would have to understand the value in updating personal data in order to share it. The company turned to birthdays to accomplish its task, creating a personalized birthday message—and song—for each of its two hundred thousand customers. Recipients were prompted to go online and enjoy a melody created just for them based on their ages, interests, location, and other data, and an animated video communicated the benefits of providing personal information.

The campaign's results accelerated as smoothly as an Audi A6. More than half of the birthday card recipients opened the initial message; 85 percent who listened to the song downloaded the melody; and 38 percent of Audi's total clients—seventy-six thousand people—updated their data.[9]

These are tangible results, yet customer equity is still rarely considered in corporate financial analyses. This will surely change as loyalty and data-driven marketing become more prevalent, but if there is one area in which marketers are not doing themselves any favors, it is in measurement. There are no generally accepted customer accounting practices and no agreement on standard return on investment calculations for customers or campaigns in the industry. Customer marketers might gravitate toward common practices, like measuring "incrementality," "prepost activity," and "test and control," but unlike the ISO 9001 designation for operations-driven companies, there are no established accounting standards for customer management.

The closest the industry has come to establishing a common customer measure has been Fred Reichheld's Net Promoter Score, which has been embraced by chief financial officers and marketers alike because of its simplicity.[10] Reichheld, a director of the business strategy firm Bain & Company, essentially boiled down all customer measures to this ultimate question: How likely is it that you would recommend this company to a friend or colleague?[11] The Net Promoter Score, while simplistic, is a critical first step in customer measurement and earning credibility from the street. Reichheld has been a pioneer in researching customer management with a direct focus on proving bottom-line results. His analysis has shown that the value of a loyal customer is significantly greater than that of a churning customer. No surprise, since there is no cost to acquire a customer who is already loyal to the company. It is less necessary to invest in retaining an existing customer than in increasing the shopping frequency or spending of a new one; engaging a new one is also more expensive. Yet in his book *The Loyalty Effect* Reichheld reports half the customers at most companies change over in five years.[12] Half!

Reichheld's analysis exposes another contradiction in customer measurement—and an area where customer marketers could up their game. While we are quick to show the CFO the financial gains buried in our customer file, we might be better served if we focused on risk. Companies are losing value on an asset that was expensive to acquire when customers leave at such an alarming rate. The cost of acquisition is an easy measure for any company to calculate. How happy would shareholders be if they recognized that the cost of customer acquisition was not paying a dividend?

Companies routinely fund capital investments in technologies that are amortized over three or more years. It only makes sense that investments in the customer asset should be measured accordingly. The investment a company makes in its loyal customers is paid back time after time, and the effort a company makes to meaningfully connect with customers and create enduring, value-based relationships has a direct bearing on the bottom line, especially when considering the higher cost of acquiring new ones.

But when it comes right down to it, the paradigm shift will be in recognizing that your success is founded in your value to the customer rather than in the customer's value to you.

What Loyalty? Is My Customer Cheating on Me?

The potential value generated by customer loyalty is a subject that has—thanks to a proliferation of programs—received a great deal of attention in recent years. Yet most organizations have little or no idea how loyal their customers are.

Those companies that do try to measure loyalty typically end up measuring customer satisfaction instead, and that can be risky. Think of customer satisfaction as the Trojan horse of loyalty: If customer satisfaction is accepted as true loyalty, which is a generous gift, then the company tricks itself into believing all is well and right between it and its customers. The scary truth, however, is that many "satisfied" customers are simply tolerating these services until they can find a competitor that offers a better price, service, or location. For every loyal customer who promotes a brand, there is another whose bags are packed, waiting for the next slightly better feature or benefit to come along—loyalty is hard earned and nurtured every day. It doesn't just come stumbling through the gate.

In fact, it's worth distinguishing up front between two kinds of loyalty: behavioral and emotional. What we deem to be satisfied customers often fall under the former. There is, of course, a third subset of shoppers who purchase a product or service strictly out of habit and with little rational assessment. McKinsey & Company refers to this level of engagement as "inertial" loyalty.[13] According to McKinsey, life insurers and utility companies are industries whose customers tend to be inertial, although insurance has pulled up its socks in recent years to assume a leadership role in customer advocacy.[14]

Recognizing that marketers are somewhat hamstrung by customer inertia, we'll focus on behavioral and emotional loyalty, where there are significant gains to be made.

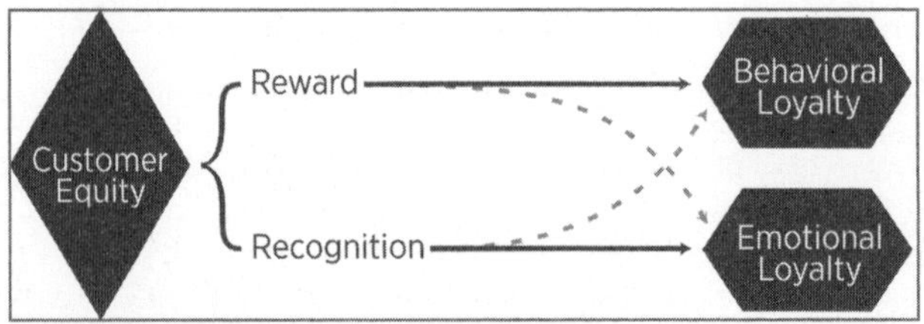

Behavioral loyalty simply reflects purchasing behavior and is typically motivated by rewards. Customers who maintain their shopping frequency and purchasing patterns are deemed loyal to the company because they shop with something close to the average consumer's spending behaviors. If asked in a survey, that customer is likely to tell you what you want to hear. Products are fine. Service is fine. Prices are fine. He or she has no bone to pick with you, but as soon as a better option is presented, that same shopper will drop you like a bag of hammers.

Behavioral loyalty is a very strong indication of convenience, price advantage, or even a lack of viable competition, but it falls short as a measure of customer engagement. Behavioral loyalty is fragile and fleeting.

Emotional loyalty, on the other hand, exists within a sustained customer relationship and is based on the company's capacity to recognize the customer's contributions directly. That customer is yours, despite very attractive offers from the competition. Most financial analysts find it difficult to conceive of a marriage of emotion and commercial results, although it is arguably the most solid measure of future customer value. Research by the Gallup Organization has been helpful, providing clear evidence that a customer who is emotionally loyal to a business is more valuable than one whose loyalty is only behavioral, or due to satisfaction. In a surprising study, researchers John Fleming and Jim Asplund found that customers of an international credit card provider who were "rationally satisfied" performed only slightly better than those who described themselves as "dissatisfied" and demonstrated nearly identical spending behavior.[15]

Emotionally satisfied customers, meanwhile, increased their spending by 67 percent over a twelve-month period compared with a mere 8 percent among those who were rationally satisfied. The data also showed that emotionally satisfied customers used their

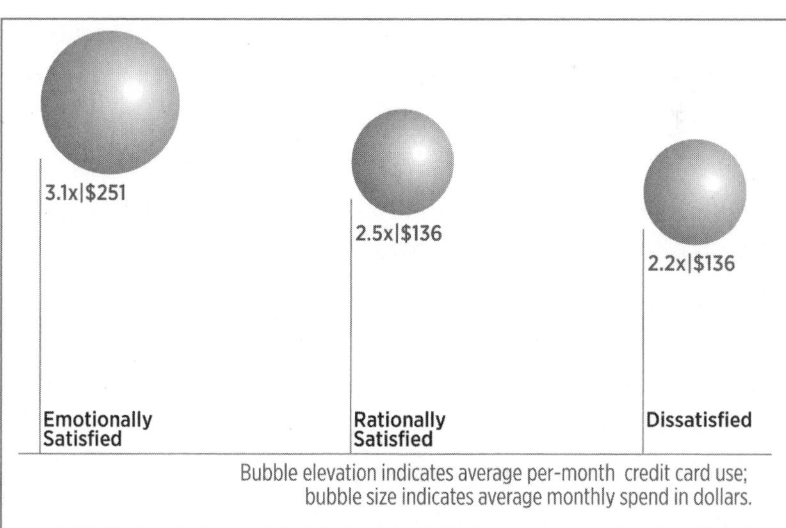

Source: Human Sigma: Managing the Employee-Customer Encounter, Gallup Press, 2007

credit cards 3.1 times per month, and spent $251 on average, while rationally satisfied customers used their cards 2.5 times a month for an average spending of $136. What's more, Gallup found that this "emotional advocacy" was alive and well across multiple consumer categories, including retail banking, hospitality, airlines, and retail.[16]

Customer Intimacy, Your Emotional Rescue

Quantifying the value of emotional loyalty is an important first step toward getting organizational alignment, but then comes the nuts and bolts of obtaining it and the organizationwide follow-through. To achieve emotional loyalty, and ultimately customer intimacy, a company needs to apply some rigor to the data collection and analysis and understand their demands, inspirations, and aspirations. Companies can benefit from advanced analytical techniques to design more relevant and meaningful communications, products, services, rewards, and experiences. These are the anchors of customer loyalty, and when done right, they drive financial performance.

It's harder than it looks but not as hard as you think. Customer behaviors are predictable, their experiences are measurable, and a dashboard of tools is available to any marketer with a reasonably robust database. The biggest hurdle at the end of the day will be strategic. Pursuing a customer-intimate strategy requires a fundamental shift of focus, from product to customer. This means getting all the functional groups involved. When beginning to map the customer journey it becomes clear that the organization needs every part that touches them to be onboard.

Although we may have a more exact measure of emotional loyalty someday, the power of today's data is highly predictive and I can safely say that we're past the point of reading tea leaves to plan customer strategy. Case in point: One of LoyaltyOne's grocery clients recently asked us why it was not selling more meat at one of its urban stores. We examined the data from the loyalty card program and identified the key customer segments of that location: college students, young singles, and low-income couples. When we recommended adding single-serve, convenient, and lower-priced cuts of meat, sales in the beef category rose 12 percent.

This strategy not only helped to prevent an underserved group of customers from seeking shopping alternatives, but it strengthened its relationship with the retailer. Such small, tactical initiatives can have a cumulative effect on customer intimacy over time.

But despite huge data stores, many companies are still conditioned to using their customer information to accelerate this week's product sales, not to map shopper needs. It's a hard habit to break. There are a few well-noted exceptions—Best Buy, Amazon, and Tesco have all built analytical engines around their customers. But most companies are still doing fairly rudimentary things with their data. And despite the best intentions of marketers to focus on the consumer, most companies find it difficult to justify the associated costs, especially when the resulting emotional loyalty is hard to measure.

Enterprise Loyalty: One Small Step for Marketing, One Giant Leap for Loyalty

Such a commitment requires more than tactical, top-down strategizing; it takes an organizationwide transformation that redirects its focus from the product to the customer. It is what we call enterprise loyalty, and it is a barrier-breaking concept. It requires releasing the power of customer data beyond the marketing department, where it is kept under wraps, and setting it free across the entire organization, from purchasing to finance and from the corporate office to the store clerk. The goal of enterprise loyalty is not simply enhancing the customer experience, but transforming it.

Customer data can inform decisions throughout the company when it becomes a shared currency, from merchandising and product design to store location, layout, and pricing. Companies that use this approach are surpassing traditional loyalty-marketing programs or one-off campaigns. They are taking a more holistic approach to the way the entire organization responds to their customers. But make no mistake: Such change can be demanding. Each business unit is committed to conventional data sets, and colleagues may not lay out the welcome mat for the idea of folding customer data into the formula. Members of the research group love their random samples; why would they want to recalibrate their tests with customer value segments? Retail merchants live and die by year-over-year measures such as same-store sales, average selling price, inventory turns, and items per basket. We will need to demonstrate the power of the data when unit and customer measures are combined. To do this there need to be some fundamental shifts across areas of operations, beginning with the adoption of an enterprisewide strategy that carries the company from a pure, product-obsessed approach to a more customer-focused operational practice.

To make my point, let's get on the ground where companies are today. Generally I see three categories.

Product Obsessed: At one end of the spectrum there are those companies whose lifeblood has been a disciplined focus on innovation and product development. These companies, such as Novartis, Intel, Sony Ericsson, and General Electric, are product specialists, and as long as they can sustain a steady stream of new product innovation that remains enough to retain competitive advantage, customer engagement will be a distant second.

Customer Committed: At the other end of the spectrum are companies like Amazon.com, Zappos.com, Gilt Groupe, and Tesco. Many of these organizations were born of the perfect combination of customer data and innovation and use customer intimacy as a strategic lever for growth.

Operational Opportunists: But most companies are not Amazon.com or Zappos.com or Tesco. They live rather in an in-between world and lack strategic focus—not due to poor management but because diversification is a risk-mitigation strategy. By keeping many balls in motion they can shift strategies at will. These companies simultaneously juggle product development, innovation, and customer tactics wherever needed. They compete on efficiency or product innovation or some combination thereof, and those with data use it sporadically to solve point-in-time issues such as customer service problems or to drive basket size, sales, or other measures. Sure, customer service and targeted campaigns will always be an arrow in their quiver, but they haven't completely integrated the customer into their strategy or into how they architect their brand experience. Because of this, operational opportunists fall short of fully vesting themselves in using customer intimacy as their strategic lever.

Making the Loyalty Leap

Assuming a company is prepared to move customers into its business equation, what steps are we really asking it to take? It's not a somersault or a backflip, but it is a clear and deliberate step, or leap, to the right.

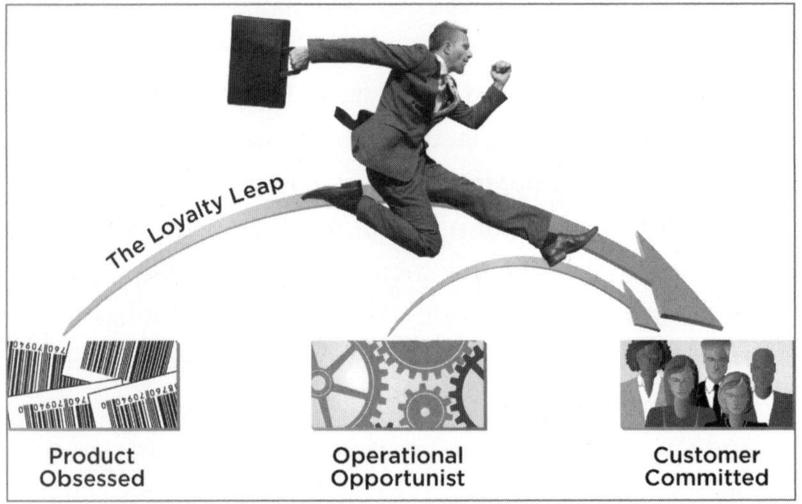

Making the Loyalty Leap demands a more systematic and disciplined approach to the use of customer data from operational opportunists than from the others; it takes a genuine commitment to transforming one-way customer channels into two-way dialogues and thinking about product innovation and operations through the customer lens. Incorporating customer data or customer-centric strategies into fundamental operations does not require tearing up the strategic floorboards. Customer commitment is just that, a commitment to making customers the heart of everything the company does.

The Loyalty Leap is also a step to the right for product obsessed organizations, but one in which design, innovation, and production have had a singular focus. It's time to open up to customer data and the innovation insight it brings.

For an example of this Loyalty Leap in motion, let's go back to the wireless communications companies discussed earlier as a product-obsessed sector that is increasingly under pressure to fix the customer experience. A handful of consumer campaigns and other as-needed tactics will not solve the service issue for these competitors, yet due to the watchful eye of the world markets, they cannot afford to abandon their product focus. These telcos are in the enviable position of being customer and communications data hubs, so they have the necessary assets to start the shift. The only thing missing is a strategic imperative to take that leap into customer management.

Operator? This Line Is Out of Service

Imagine the possibilities. Your local phone provider has data about both your home phone service and your media habits, which come from your cable service. It has a picture of your Web activity, including your home page, preferred Web sites, and time-of-day usage behaviors. Add your wireless calling patterns, data usage, favorite apps, cell phone payment patterns, and—in a number of geographies—whether you are using your phone for cell phone payments. On top of that, you have a service relationship with the company since all those devices are in constant need of TLC. Its service workers may even have been to your house if they provide other telecommunications services, such as cable.

For your phone and Internet provider to place you at the heart of its mission it would simply need to undergo a shift. It starts with a disciplined focus on mapping your journey, mining your data, and creating meaningful experiences—but none of this detracts from its ability to deliver on its core product and service agreements. In fact, if it used your data to inform its product innovation, it might create a better product experience as well!

This brings to mind the daughter of a close friend who is enrolled at McGill University in Montreal. She's squarely in the telco target segment of youth, age fourteen to twenty-five, who are huge data and device users. Her phone is a necessity, right up there with food and shelter.

Now, there is nothing a nineteen-year-old girl hates more than changing her phone number and her contacts, especially when she moves to a new city where she knows no one. And yet her phone provider cannot figure out a way to reserve her phone number in her hometown or her number in Montreal. This may not be an issue in other markets, but it serves to remind us that the world is full of these types of frustrating customer experiences. So over her four years in college, moving back and forth each year, she has had eight phone numbers, and in each case she had to switch all her contacts. Why is it so hard for a company that can launch a new phone device every six weeks to create a decent phone experience for its target customer?

Because as long as product-obsessed companies maintain their competitive advantage they have little reason to sharpen their focus on customers. I sense there's an inherent belief that you're either born into customer focus, like many of the online players, or you can only get there by taking your company and its share price down the bumpy road of radical change. Operational opportunists are more passive-aggressive in their outlook, which tends to be on a three-year plan and never among immediate priorities. I've heard everything from "This is year of the Web site" to "We're business-casing a data warehouse," and of course my favorite "We're exploring social media." These are tactics, but make no mistake: They are not stand-ins for systematic customer engagement.

The shifts for the operational opportunist or the product obsessed are not cataclysmic. It is really just a leap of faith—faith in the ability to better serve customers by placing them at the center of the organization's purpose. It is about unwavering commitment to a strategy and changing the lens through which the company evaluates its decisions. Only by this path will companies reap the full benefits of customer intimacy, and in the process provide the enriched services and products that will ensure a distinct point of engagement; one wherein customers become emotionally, and unmistakably, vested in the brand.

CHAPTER 4

Customer Loyalty Versus Customer Intimacy: Is There Really a Difference?

Being customer committed takes most companies a king-sized dedication to understanding the many ways their customers use their brand. Take the Hilton hospitality chain. Years ago Hilton retained Epsilon to build and manage the capabilities behind its long-standing Hilton HHonors Program, an initiative that touches more than twenty-five million people globally. Every year roughly two million people sign up for the HHonors program through the Web, a hotel, or a customer service agent.

Hilton has been able to keep its long-standing HHonors program fresh and growing by continuously refining its messaging and its offers. Through continued customer data mining and campaign measurement Hilton realized a few years ago that each of its members joined for a unique reason, so there were distinct groups of customers whose motivations, goals, and preferences varied significantly. Some guests preferred special offers, for example, while others wanted upgrades or frequent travel points.

Hotels have always known that the check-in experience is the moment of truth in the guest experience. It's their first touch with the customer, a chance to establish a human connection, to communicate programs and services, and to deliver outstanding service. It's also the optimal stage in the customer journey to gather detailed data. But with only a few minutes for guest check-in, the experience has got to be flawless. Hilton engaged Epsilon to develop a customer-management solution.

And it did. Epsilon's SONAR application became the new industry standard, not just for collecting data but for delivering personalized guest messages based on individual purchase preferences—at the front desk and afterward, through a series of personalized e-mails between stays. Hilton now engages members by asking them how they prefer to earn and use rewards, where they travel, and whether it's vacation, business, or a short stay. They inquire about their guests' travel-related interests, such as golfing, theater, or health, and their hotel brand preferences, including DoubleTree, Hampton Inn, or Embassy Suites.

Hilton could segment its customers and personalize the details of their experience with this information. It also tailors unique messages and offers for these members using SONAR, with more than fifty new ones added every month.

In turn, the guest's spending history at the hotel—from the number of stays to rewards earned to whether or not they used the minibar—is stored in a central database and can be retrieved at the front desk during check-in. The system uses advanced algorithms automatically to check the guest's profile against hundreds of variables to recommend the best offers in rank order. For a first-time guest, the agent would likely focus on informational messages, such as where to find the gym, the restaurant hours, and local shopping. If he or she is a guest who recently stayed at the DoubleTree in Minneapolis, the desk clerk can see that he or she used Wi-Fi and was randomly upgraded, prompting an opportunity to up-sell to a suite.

The magic of this recommendation engine is that guest checks are carried out in real time, and they shape the guest experience. It is effective because booking agents and front-desk employees have the right history and the right recommendations at their fingertips. They just need to personalize the delivery so the experience never feels awkward or mechanistic.

This magic has delivered outstanding results. Hilton's personalized communications received 50 percent higher open and click-through rates than previous marketing campaigns that lacked the intimacy feature. The hotel saw a 5 percent lift in member spending, which translates to top-line revenue. And along the way the Hilton brands realized improved activation and engagement rates.

The added bonus: Hilton HHonors can straddle the fine line of privacy by using groundbreaking technology to create more relevant messages and customer data to deliver meaningful offers without compromising its members' confidence in the brand.

So Is a Loyalty Program Built on Intimacy or on Intimate Customer Data?

Hilton's HHonors is considered among the best in class for hotel loyalty programs, but there are a lot of programs out there. In fact, according to loyalty-marketing industry publisher COLLOQUY, the average U.S. household belongs to more than 18 loyalty programs, even though each is only active in 8.4.[1] This popularity of consumer loyalty programs then makes it worth taking a closer look at the relationship between intimacy and loyalty.

First, we should clear up any potential confusion about the meaning of loyalty. We generally understand loyalty as what we consider faithfulness: to a mate, a political ideal, a favorite sports team, and so forth. A commitment is made when loyalty is pledged to stand by even when setbacks occur or the team loses miserably. Traditional wedding vows include a promise to stay together "for better, for worse, for richer, for poorer." Die-hard sports fans stick with their teams through winning streaks and shellackings, sometimes enduring years of losing seasons.

Loyalty in a business context suggests the same kind of faithfulness, even in the face of other choices. In the last chapter we considered behavioral and emotional loyalty. Recall that behavioral loyalty, like "customer satisfaction," can lull a company into a false sense of complacency. A customer who feels only behavioral loyalty is likely to walk away from a brand as soon as a better offer comes along. A customer with emotional loyalty, on the other hand, wants to stay true to the brand, and will ride out the hard times even when a competitor offers him or her a better option. A truly loyal customer is one who will seek out a company and prefer to do business with it again and again.

We all want customer loyalty, of course. Who wouldn't? But what's the real value of customer loyalty? How does it affect a business over the long haul? It's not a squishy concept. There is real value in customer loyalty that creates a natural exit barrier. Customers choosing to leave a company they've been doing business with abandon long-established relationships with its employees, and they walk away from the investment it made in data and building a customer history. Most important, they exit the balance sheet, and that company will undoubtedly spend more to bring them back than to acquire a new one.

But if an organization has used that knowledge effectively to create value and positive experiences for the customers, they are much more likely to stay. The more that is known about the consumer, and the deeper the relationship, the higher the barrier to exit.

The term "loyalty" is also often used as a shorthand expression for customer loyalty programs. A loyalty program is an elegant way for a company to engage its customers in conversation but there is a big difference between simply choosing to launch a loyalty program and having a commitment to developing true customer loyalty. An exceptional loyalty program is one that moves well beyond the simple act of rewarding purchase activity to one where the customer is engaged in an explicit relationship, where there are rewards for behaviors that benefit both parties. It is a customer contract of sorts, and not to be taken lightly, as these customers are usually the best performers and most engaged with the company's brand. While loyalty programs alone do not cultivate customer intimacy, the most effective ones are tailor-made for this purpose.

If you need evidence that consumers see value in loyalty programs, then chew on this: North American loyalty memberships rose to more than two billion by 2010, from less than one billion in 2000.[1]

So what exactly is the relationship between loyalty and intimacy, and are they different? To put it simply, customer intimacy is a means to the end, to that goal of creating emotional loyalty with customers. Delivering a meaningful service proposition to the customer creates intimacy, and therefore a clear competitive advantage in the marketplace. Loyalty, particularly emotional loyalty, happens when you get everything right, and the customer is committed "for richer, for poorer. . . ." There is a ladder effect: Loyalty programs are an explicit means to elevate customer intimacy, and customer intimacy can be the precursor to emotional loyalty, which is the basis for customer profitability.

But Do I Have to Dangle Incentives to Win Customer Intimacy?

Must you have a loyalty program to build customer intimacy? The short answer is no, but it's a pretty good idea, because the loyalty program creates the perfect ecosystem for gathering the necessary data to better understand and serve your customers.

That said, there are a number of industries that thrive without loyalty programs. Home insurers, for example, achieve intimacy by using home inspections to provide value-added advice on in-home hazards for their policyholders. Some banks strive for local relationships, going to great lengths to greet their patrons by name and ask if they have any questions about their mortgages or other products. These customer-intimate practices work whether or not rewards are offered, because the players are already able to track customer behavior and use it to form a longitudinal view of their interactions. The data advises them on what to say or do during customer-facing activities.

Loyalty programs, meanwhile, provide the kind of detailed data that inform in-store strategies and employee decisions around the customer. Implementing a loyalty program can serve as a kind of statement of purpose, guiding a company's efforts toward customer intimacy. That is if the data is gathered and deployed in a way that is systematic and strategic. But if the company is considering the pursuit of loyalty—and, more specifically, points programs—as a panacea for its troubles, it should think again. If a loyalty program relies on rewards, points, or discounts alone, as the sole means of affecting customer loyalty, it will connect with only a small and often fickle group of customers. This tactical tool set will not remedy company missteps or engender the type of behavioral change associated with true loyalty. Even the best designed programs will not compensate for a poorly conceived or executed business strategy.

A loyalty program is but one tool, albeit a very effective one because it is a data mechanism that works across all of your channels and sifts out your best customers. But a loyalty program is most effective when it's serving the greater purpose of building customer commitment.

Unfortunately, many companies are awkward in the way they collect and use loyalty data. They obtain customers' contact information with the promise of targeted messages and rewards and then use the file to bombard them with untargeted promotions.

We've all been there, providing personal information in-store and online because we want access to that article or the free refill, and then regretting it for the sheer volume of messages that litter our in-box. What you've experienced is not a loyalty program; it's bad business.

When we help companies design a loyalty program or have them join the AIR MILES coalition, we spend a significant amount of time educating clients on the basic consumer contracts they are entering, among other logistics of a successful initiative. On the customer's side there is an agreement to share information about purchasing habits in exchange for some form of incremental, relevant value. On the company's side there is a commitment to use the information to explicitly tailor offers, communications, and experiences to suit that customer, while also capitalizing on customer intimacy and creating stronger enterprise value.

Good-bye Stranger: Making Connections with the Three Vs

A company must first win meaningful customer engagement in order to build the right loyalty program. It needs to achieve what I call the "three Vs" of loyalty: value, visibility, and voice.

Any loyalty program needs the first V, value, just to get off the ground. Value is that sparkling object that attracts customers, and it is a requirement for an information exchange. Customers are inherently skeptical when merchants ask them for their phone number or zip code. It breeds suspicion. Second, the customer is justifiably uncomfortable sharing information when there is no expectation of getting anything in return. The age-old practice of giving retail customers 10 percent off their first purchase is a good first step, because it drives up acquisitions. But it doesn't necessarily speak to the value that the program itself will bring long term. However, if the retailer consistently delivers on the value promise, and gives its customers a perceived value that's commensurate with their increasing spending, then it can reasonably expect to keep them for life. Our AIR MILES program, for instance, has millions of consumers forming the consistently loyal base that has been collecting for more than twenty years.

The importance of a customer's continued participation leads us to the second V, visibility. The core purpose of a loyalty program is to develop a deep understanding of customer dynamics. The program must attract a sufficient level of participation so that the organization can track those customers who collectively account for a significant portion of its sales volume. If this can be done on a sustained basis, the transactional history and the customer's journey can be mapped, creating a viable business asset. Marketers that limit themselves by working with discrete data sets, using campaign or research data, miss the big picture. In essence, this information, while helpful, exists in a vacuum. Working with spotty data is a little like watching a movie trailer in which you know the stars and whether it is a comedy or an action film, but you have no idea what the story is. But through today's technical capabilities, devices like loyalty programs provide an in-the-moment analysis of customer transactions that when combined with a longitudinal view of their activity permit the company to examine behaviors at a higher level of detail.

Marketers can conduct meaningful research with this information, and monitor the social sphere to identify the motivations behind customer actions. But if a loyalty program has low visibility, and represents just 10 percent to 20 percent penetration of the customer base, for instance, the data set may be too limited for analysis.

The final V is for voice—creating a platform for communications with your customers. Voice may be the most critical asset for attaining engagement in the modern age of social media and collaborative brand development. We've seen the dangers a brand can face when channels of communication between a company and its customers aren't fully open, or when the brand is unable to provide even the most basic level of contact management. I had a recent experience managing my home phone account. Already a good customer, I had made the decision to consolidate my wireless, cable, Internet, and home phone accounts to get that "best customer" deal it kept promising. So I signed up at $39.95 per month and thought I was done. But in the four weeks that followed, I received at least a dozen offers for the service I already had. Two of them stood out. One offered the package at $29.95, and the second arrived a week later offering the services for $24.95.

So let's see: If I took the lowest offer, I would have saved $15 per month, or $180 in a year. When you multiply that experience times millions of now very unhappy "best" customers, you really see what we mean by revenue at risk.

Indeed, voice, or the permission to speak openly to your loyalty members, is a powerful tool and should be used for more than communications about the next bonus offer. This is the play to innovate. Members can be invited into research groups, to tweet with the president, and to advise on the navigation of your Web site. Engage them in social media but recognize that its anonymity and its free-form nature result in unstructured data that is limited in its use. On the other hand, loyalty membership can be used to encourage customers to identify themselves in all your channels. Only then can you address their issues on a customer level.

Our experience at LoyaltyOne has shown that when the three Vs are in place and working properly, customers readily embrace loyalty programs. Some of our partner merchants had an aversion to the idea of creating customized offers for customers in the early days of loyalty management. They had worked hard at the operational level to create a consistent experience for all customers and feared raucous conversations in checkout lines, where customers would compare offers and exit en masse. They didn't count on the fact that AIR MILES members expected to get custom offers because they knew they all shopped differently. It became common knowledge that customers who spent more with a particular merchant would get better offers.

I suspect this practice came from airline reward programs, in which the haves routinely beat out the have-nots, and millions of travelers make it their life's purpose to get on the upgrade list. Whatever the reason, there is no question that today's customers take the best practices from one industry and readily transpose them to another. Customers are far more sophisticated today than even a decade ago, and most of them are more than happy to participate in a loyalty program that operates transparently, offers them real benefits, and treats them with respect.

What If I Want to Invite My Friends Along?

If loyalty programs are a sophisticated way to develop deeper ties with the consumer, then coalition loyalty programs—in which groups of companies band together to offer customers a common "reward currency" and create a shared database—is loyalty on steroids. It is a collaboration of dozens, or even scores, of retailers, airlines, banks, and other organizations all operating under one program—through one card—that allows members to earn their points wherever they want, and then to redeem them however they want. A member might earn fifty thousand points through travel but prefer to redeem them for a pair of ECCO walking shoes. When done right, everyone wins, which is why a coalition model is operating in almost every major consumer market in the world. For now, unfortunately, it's not being used in the United States, where market regionality has made it challenging.

It is not a new idea, but it leverages the best practices of business partnerships to create a number of shared assets, not the least of which is access to a huge shared pool of qualified prospects. By working together, coalition partners enjoy the benefits of a larger body of data. Their customers in turn accumulate points at an accelerated pace and have access to a more diverse selection of rewards.

So let's apply the three Vs to coalition loyalty. The model enhances the value of loyalty programs because customers can be rewarded faster. How? Because the common currency (the points or miles) in a coalition program is accumulated from a wider range of spending activities and partners. This in turn accelerates the earning potential for the customer. We know, for instance, that collecting enough points for a free flight would generally take less than half as much time through a coalition program than through a credit card–only points scheme. Meantime, sponsors in the coalition can use their richer database to generate more targeted and relevant marketing activities.

The basic premise of the shared database and cost infrastructure also enables each company to devote more energy to understanding its customers and developing the relationships that matter, using the funds and resources gained from the efficiencies of the coalition model to fuel the growth.

Visibility also is raised in a coalition environment. Companies are able to better understand their customers, which products they buy, how frequently, and where. A company has visibility because the database is shared, and not only into its own customers; it can also understand the behavior of noncustomers—those patrons of other coalition members who may live across the street but choose not to enter its store.

Last, a coalition model can amplify the company's voice in customer relationships. The conversation is much richer when companies from a variety of industries are involved, and the opportunities for communication multiply. What's more, twenty years of campaign response rates and more than one hundred partners confirm that communications from a coalition, whether in print or online, have higher open and read rates than those from single-business loyalty programs. LoyaltyOne's open rates are almost twice the industry standard for retailers. And let's not forget the halo effect: Members of coalition programs are more likely to do business with other companies in the same program. Bank of Montreal, Canada's oldest lender, gives a close to home example. A few years back, in an effort to measure customer engagement, it sent out two kinds of mailers. One included bonus offers only at its retail banks, while the other expanded them to include other coalition members, including Shell and Holiday Inn. The coalition mailer's response rate was 13 percent higher than that of the solo mailer, while the cost per responder was 26 percent lower.

The coalition environment acts like a hothouse for participating companies, powerfully augmenting the effectiveness of each organization's marketing activities. Coalition members broaden their brand footprint by going to market with a variety of leaders from other market categories. Further, the richness of the data obtained from customer spending across categories enhances the ability of each participating company to fine-tune its marketing and communications strategies and ultimately acquire new customers.

At AIR MILES we have experienced what we call the multiplier, or "network," effect that exemplifies such value. This shows that the more coalition partners a consumer patronizes, the more money he or she will spend at the company that first brought the customer into the program (what we call the "originating sponsor").

Say the originating sponsor is a drugstore chain, and the customer purchases pharmaceuticals and related items at only its stores. For the purpose of comparison, say that person spends $100 at one store in that chain. If the same person does business with two other companies from the chain's loyalty coalition, then he or she is also likely to increase his or her spending in that drugstore chain, to $125. Basically, the person is increasing the purchases made within the coalition in an effort to earn more reward currency from each participating merchant. Now if he or she patronizes five merchants in the loyalty coalition, then the shopper would spend even more among those merchants.

But it is not about spending more money—overall, consumers are not. They are simply consolidating more of their purchases within the coalition partners to earn more rewards.

The AIR MILES customer is clearly demonstrating a change in behavior as she frequents more sponsors and becomes more entrenched, and finally more emotionally engaged, in the program. The appeal of rewards encourages the customer to consolidate her spending among companies that offer the same currency or reward

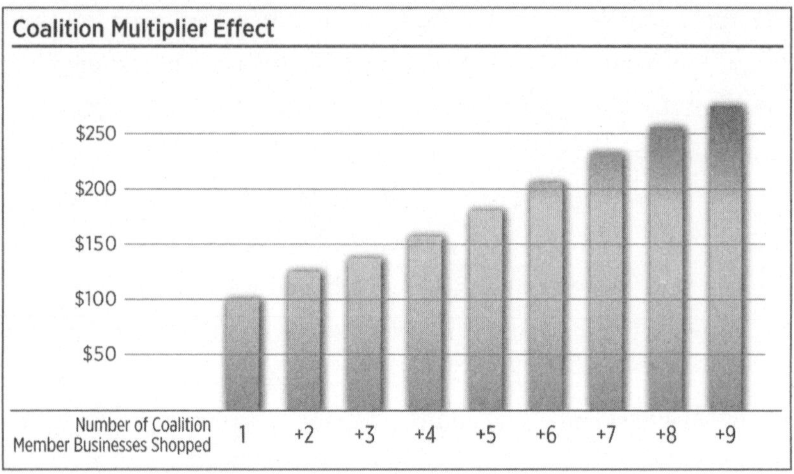

miles for her business. The network becomes a vibrant community of activity in which organizations respond to the cues they receive from observed customer behavior and provide relevant communications and offers, proactively managing the relationship with each specific customer.

Connecting Through the Three Rs of Loyalty

If a loyalty coalition is a vibrant community, then the relationship between a company and its customer is a collaborative bond, one fostered through meaningful and well-timed communications and recognition. We need to return to the basic principles that drive behavioral and emotional loyalty and the role loyalty programs play in ensuring this kind of partnership.

For me, a successful loyalty initiative requires a deft execution of the "three Rs" of loyalty: reward, recognition, and relevance.

Reward is the tangible exchange of value (discounts or points) that occurs when the consumer purchases goods or services from organizations using his or her loyalty card or identifier. Rewards are a simple way to give something back to your customers and to say thank you for their continued patronage. More important, customers expect them.

As a result, rewards are usually, though not always, tied to what we call "hard benefits": points, miles, a discount, or something provided for free. "Soft benefits," on the other hand, are intangible or experiential perks that a company can provide to its customers that do not directly relate to product cost or future value, such as VIP tickets to an event.

Despite the fact that I lead one of the largest loyalty program providers in the world, the truth is that rewards get you behavioral loyalty; you need to identify and then build on what customers love about you to engage them in a way that creates an emotional bond. Rewards are often easily duplicated in today's competitive environment and leave a company vulnerable to rivals with incrementally better benefits. If I use my MasterCard enough, for instance, I'll qualify for a free flight on American Airlines. But if I live in London and my new Visa Signature card offers a quicker way to accumulate miles on British Airways, I'm likely to switch my purchases to the Visa in pursuit of the promised reward. As long as the status quo looks like a better deal to me, I'll stay. The moment something better comes along, I'm likely to abandon my current program.

That said, rewards have the potential to create emotional loyalty when marketed properly and used in the right circumstances. Imagine a situation where your frequent flier miles could enable your grandmother to fly in for the holidays or for an important birthday. Assuming your terms and conditions do not bar little old ladies from flying during high season, the reward transcends its role as a reinforcement of consumer behavior. I heard it said once that kids remember their parents for the times they acted out of character and bent the rules, like when they allowed dessert for breakfast. This kind of reward delivers a positive experience that the consumer will long remember and equate with your company.

Such required give-and-take helps to reinforce the old 80-20 Rule, formally known as the Pareto Principle. The Pareto Principle basically states that 80 percent of the effects come from 20 percent of the causes. In commerce this means that 80 percent of your sales will likely be generated by 20 percent of your customers. We have found that the 80-20 Rule doesn't quite mathematically work in all categories, but the effect does exist among our clients in a number of sectors, in areas where they see a definitive concentration in the spending of their best customers. The grocery, pharmacy, and petroleum sectors, as well as other high-frequency retail outlets, have found that the top 10 percent of customers represent around 50 percent of sales. When we look at the next 10 percent of best customers, that spending figure reaches 60 percent to 80 percent of sales.

This concentration of spending can reach the absurd in some industries. Take for instance the social networking and online gaming company Tagged, which reported that the top 1 percent of its players accounted for 46 percent of its gaming revenue for the first six months of 2011.[2] The point is, heightened engagement with customers leads them to increase their interactions with the company, and to tell others about it as well.

Once the best customers are identified through the shared data of the loyalty program, it is time to recognize them. Recognition consists of gestures that say, "We appreciate you for giving us your business." Oftentimes the most effective forms of recognition are delivered through intangible, or soft, benefits.

The best benefit portfolio should balance hard, or currency-based, benefits with soft, or experiential, benefits. The latter could be access to the airline lounge, faster check-in at the hotel, or VIP tickets to an event. In fact, based on a six-month test of reward effectiveness by COLLOQUY, which it reported in a white paper in 2005, those members who received both hard and soft reward offers had returned value scores that were 10 percentage points higher than those of benchmarked members.[3]

Travel loyalty programs are designed to deliver recognition rewards. Whether you're collecting for planes, trains, automobiles, or hotels, the customer contract remains the same: Use our services more often and we will treat you special. As a road warrior myself, I would trade all my points for special treatment. The reason? Despite their shopping malls and restaurants, airports can be horrible places. I want to spend as little time as possible in an airport, and when I'm there I need to be productive and efficient, or if I'm exhausted, I want to unplug and rest. Express-line privileges and lounges with Internet access are critical to creating a positive experience.

And I'm not alone. Many of my compadres will game the system to accumulate enough flight segments or points to maintain "super-duper platinum" status. Going to Dubai through L.A.? Some customers will actually book obscure flight routes toward the end of each year just to make sure they qualify for top-tier recognition.

Recognition benefits are where luxury retailers become very inventive. A sales associate at the Saks Fifth Avenue store in Houston catalogued the closets of his very best clients and recommended what to wear, what to store, and what to throw out. If you are a premier customer with American Express you get offers to attend major events, such as tennis tournaments and concerts. Nordstrom concierge services assist with party planning, sending flowers, or making dinner recommendations and reservations. And GameStop's PowerUp Rewards offers paid-tier members the chance to win VIP access to the Comic-Con International convention, tickets to a NASCAR race, and a trip to Rome to visit the sites from the game Assassin's Creed.

In short, recognition starts with identifying your best customers, learning what makes them tick, creating individualized recognition items, and then saying thank you on a regular basis.

It's this realization that often motivates a company to launch a loyalty program. The underlying desire is to provide value-added benefits that propel the customer to commit his or her continued loyalty to the company. The problem is that while most loyalty initiatives hold the promise of delivering a customer-intimate strategy, they are too often executed at the most basic level. In other words, most programs simply use rewards to coerce consumers into sharing more information while continuing to speak to them through mass channels with the same one-size-fits-all messaging.

Rewards and recognition are just the basic components of the loyalty strategy. The key is to evolve beyond merely identifying and rewarding great customers and to recognize all of the critical touch points where you can connect with them in ways that show you understand who they are and what they care about. This is the third R, relevance, and it represents the most powerful opportunity for companies to create deep emotional loyalty from their customers.

Unfortunately, achieving relevance is an increasingly daunting task. As traditional channels of communication continue to splinter and be sidelined by emerging mediums, such as social and mobile media, the process of connecting with the consumer also faces fragmentation. So how do you break through? The only message that will rise above the noise in this environment is the one that recognizes the consumers' needs and offers a solution.

Think about relevance in terms of context plus content. Content for targeted segments is easy, but content alone won't win the day. Offers and messaging should be framed in a contextual environment that makes sense and actually engages customers and gets them to pay attention. Our work with high-frequency retailers has shown us that placing the same offer in a relevant contextual environment can more than double the incremental margin generated from each customer.

But What Will Put Relevance to Work? How? And for Whom?

The most sophisticated and successful loyalty programs are organized around a relevance strategy. But in this case contextual relevance is managed across the continuum of multiple customer interactions, spanning a few years or more. Like most customer-management strategies, the process starts with segmentation, to define the target audience. Creating this kind of multilayer segmentation strategy involves a delicate balancing act. It must be sufficiently granular so that the goals will be achieved but not so complex that campaigns become too onerous to execute reasonably.

The first step in implementing this strategy requires exploration of the question: Who are my customers? This segmentation should identify not only the customer's current value to the enterprise, but also his potential value in the future. Customers should be segmented based on their observed shopping behavior, including everything from the products they purchase to the channels and store formats they frequent. When this analysis is combined with demographic information, a meaningful picture of those customers who are strong potential targets will emerge.

Understanding "who" will naturally lead to the exploration of "how." The how is again about creating the contextual environment for the company's messages so that the target consumer will pay attention to what he or she is sent. We must find messages that strike consumers as relevant to their own needs and desires versus generalized communications that are geared to the masses. The analytic results could focus the company's attention on demographics (for instance, mothers with children), purchasing behaviors (organized around healthy eating or product profiling), specific ethnicities, or perhaps a combination of all three. Once we recognize the who, we can begin to understand how best to communicate with our customers.

The last segmentation element to consider is the "what." The what defines the key motivators that will influence consumer behavior by answering several pertinent questions: Will discounts work better than points? Which channels of communication are most effective? And are there special benefits or opportunities that will be more motivating to the consumer than others?

The formula for creating relevance exists in combining these three forms of segment marketing in such a way that the consumer responds favorably to the message, resulting in a more profitable and effective campaign.

An apt example comes from how we use shopper data to inform profitable merchandising and marketing decisions when we run our analytics at LoyaltyOne. Using our Precima model for comprehensive customer understanding around multidimensional segmentation, we score customers across three profitability dimensions: value (who the shopper is, based on sales and margin potential); solutions (how they shop and what they buy); and impact (what marketing they respond to).

Say the father in a target family recently discovered he has a heart disease. This major event changes his lifestyle dramatically, and his wife looks at food shopping in a whole different way. Though she still makes the traditional dishes her mother taught her, she has begun to substitute healthier alternatives for some ingredients. Every time she visits the supermarket her purchases tell a story and identify her as a shopper interested in longevity. In response, her supermarket begins to customize offers around her new purchasing choices to include recipes, healthy lifestyle tips, and coupons for products she is likely to buy, such as nuts and grains.

Our experience with a variety of clients has demonstrated the who, how, and what at work; the strategy uses complex systems to cobble together a complete picture of the customer through individual shopping trips. Indeed, by communicating directly to the consumer with such relevant messaging, we found a retailer's incremental profit margin more than doubled.[4]

No Doubt About It: Loyalty Is a Matter of Trust

Loyalty programs offer companies a flexible and powerful way to cultivate customer intimacy. Unfortunately, surprisingly few companies are doing a good job at it. One lesson we have learned is that there is a significant difference between the experiences executives think they are delivering and the perceptions of those encounters among their customers. A recent study from Accenture measured this gap, providing quantitative evidence that supports our theory. In the study 55 percent of executives rated their ability to target consumers and provide them with relevant experiences as either "ideal" or "very good." When consumers were asked whether the same companies were good at providing them with tailored, relevant experiences, only 21 percent agreed. The Accenture study involved interviews with eight hundred directors and senior managers at blue chip companies across multiple industries in the United States, Canada, China, Brazil, and other countries.

If these companies aren't getting it right, and it's pretty clear they're not, then very few are. The research also found that more than half the companies surveyed didn't take advantage of analytics to help them target, service, or interact with customers. When the most successful companies are falling short in this way, it seems to me we have a critical gap that can be turned into a significant opportunity. It's a little like teenage sex: Everybody talks about it, but few are doing it, and those who are aren't doing it very well.

The opportunity, of course, is to use data to deliver the kind of service or product proposition that sets the company apart from all the others. Doing this will build trust, gain relevance—which is not that easy—and finally realize customer loyalty and intimacy.

The real strength of relevance as an engagement strategy is that it encourages customers to stay, sharply increasing market retention and staving off competitors. Consumers implicitly understand that there is value in the data and history that they choose to share with companies. In an environment where this data is used to create a relevant experience, it would be a challenge for any competitor to replicate what that consumer has shared with the company over time, and to offer the resulting customized experience. It gets back to building emotional loyalty to support long-term, sustainable revenue streams from these customers, to evolve the long-term value and equity of the business.

But before implementing that relevance strategy, you'll need to knock on a few doors.

CHAPTER 5

The Four Doors to Relevance: What Are the Keys to Unlocking Opportunity?

For most companies, especially large organizations, reaching the customer and gaining relevance means using customer data to pass through many metaphorical doors—the door to her behavior, the door to her values, the door to her heart. Ironically, it seems that the last door anyone thinks of is the door to her house.

But an example of a company not taking full advantage of its data did recently hit home for me, literally. In fact, it was in front of my TV. You see, my wife and I are big basketball fans, as are our children. So of course we stayed home for several nights to watch the 2011 NBA finals.

Within five minutes of the end of the critical game six, the final game, my wife received an e-mail alert from the NBAStore.com, a site we regularly visit and shop. The message included an exclusive offer: The new Dallas Mavericks Champions Collection is already available at the NBAStore.com! We could place our order right there and then and be among the first to wear Dallas Maverick Champion T-shirts, hats, or other apparel.

I had to hand it to the NBAStore.com for nailing the timing of its message. But there was one critical problem with its execution: We—my whole family—are not especially fans of either of the teams playing in the finals, although my daughter is a fan of Dwyane Wade, the six-foot-four, 220-pound guard for the Miami Heat. In fact, if the NBAStore.com had tracked and cross-referenced our purchasing data, it would have noted that while we did once buy a WNBA basketball online, we had also purchased a Dwyane Wade game jersey at its physical store in New York.

The NBAStore.com did manage to capture our attention by recognizing that we had basketball on the brain, but it did not cross the threshold to full engagement, because it failed to connect with our individual preferences. It did not account for the possibility of my family being Miami Heat fans, and it risked losing future purchases, since the Heat had just lost and the NBAStore.com's offerings rubbed it in. The NBAStore.com had relied on only one of the four critical elements to establish relevance, and as a result it ran the risk of losing our long-term loyalty.

I have forgiven NBAStore.com, but your business might not be so lucky. It's essential to establish personal relevance to break through the customer noise. Your communications, your offers, everything your company does must hit a resonant chord that aligns with the customer's values, lifestyle, and needs. We've covered the steps required to establish emotional loyalty versus behavioral loyalty, and then how to use them as stepping-stones to a profitable loyalty plan—for a loyalty program has to be directly attributable to the bottom line to make financial sense. Data is your road map in this process, and the challenge is knowing which data to collect and how to use it effectively to ensure that you balance content and context.

After all, data comes in many forms, and it can be sliced and diced to reveal a lot of unexpected aspects of a consumer's loyal behavior. Data yields the clues to travel patterns, product preferences, price sensitivities, and lifestyle choices. Customer profiles are not always what you think. A shopper who buys earth-friendly clothing detergent may also drive a giant SUV. A major basketball fan watching the finals may actually be pulling for the losing team. Thankfully the information is likely already at your fingertips, the tools are accessible, and people are pretty much willing to share it. Companies just need to master the combination, and then use it responsibly. Unfortunately, the extent to which companies are unable to crack that combination is discouraging.

These Doors Are Framed by Windows of Opportunity

In a 2009 study by COLLOQUY, 68 percent of U.S. consumers rated the effectiveness of their loyalty program communications as an eight or lower, on a scale of one to ten. Said another way, only 32 percent of those surveyed thought their loyalty program communications were really hitting their mark.

As direct marketers, we know the people responding to these surveys. An average 3 percent response rate to direct communications represents the remaining 97 percent. So if you're satisfied building loyalty with only 3 percent of your customers, then keep doing what you're doing. But to make a case for deepening the loyalty of some or all of them, read on.

I won't preach the overused gospel of "the right message at the right time and in the right place," but without striking a chord with customers, a company cannot get the conversation started. And the path to relevance lies not beyond one magic door but beyond four, all of which reveal insights that can be used at different times or in the aggregate.

These doors open to reveal four key behavioral dimensions of the consumer that together will make the company's message STIC:

- **spatial**, which refers to the physical location;
- **temporal**, which in its most basic sense means timing, but which can also be expanded to include elements such as stage of life;
- **individual**, which reflects the consumer's unique personal interests, passions, and values; and
- **cultural** or **cohort**, which points to religion, causes, ethnicities, and any ongoing activities that regularly group people together.

I wish these four doors were entirely my invention, but they are not. A variation first ran in an article published in COLLOQUY'S biannual magazine, *Enterprise Loyalty in Practice* by university professors Kyle Murray and Mark Vandenbosch.[1] But I would like to elevate the four-door theory a bit, because I see it as the framework to a much more ambitious strategy. For instance, while Murray and Vandenbosch suggest that the fourth door should open onto the behavioral dimension of *channels,* I would go further and submit that it should lead to the more spectral one of *cultural* influences.

Beyond these four doors lies the journey to emotional loyalty that can only be reached through relevance.

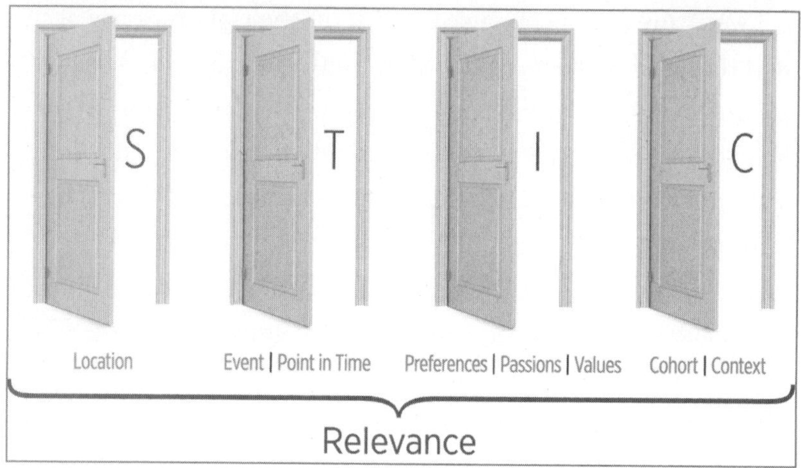

What Do I Need to Take Along?

But before we go too much further we're going to have to make a pit stop to upgrade your technical understanding of customer-data management. This takes a complexity of insights that requires more tactical work than what we covered in previous chapters, so I will spare you the owner's manual on message prioritization, recommendation engines, real-time lead generation, and the myriad of other tools in the marketer's kit. But I believe you will need a layman's understanding of customer-data management to appreciate the value of relevance. Through data algorithms, for instance, a company can run individual customer profiles against hundreds of offers to filter out which ones best meet the needs of that shopper. Algorithms make it possible for next-door neighbors to get completely different marketing offers from the same merchant, yet each one hits home.

Other tools, such as online real-time tracking through the use of cookies, can identify where a consumer is—physically and psychically—within milliseconds of when he gets online. It could determine, for instance, if he is a hiking enthusiast with financial interests and a Saturday night reservation for sushi. This cookie, which is attached to that consumer, is then auctioned off through an ad exchange to interested buyers.

Clearly there are data geeks out there who make these practices their life's purpose, and tracking relevance can become a sport. Witness my friend who uses two computers and receives completely different ad streams on each even when reviewing the exact same Web page. The reason: He uses one of his computers strictly for his financial services business and the other for his personal interests.

Wow! Should I Pack a Bigger Bag?

Tools are tools, and they are only as good as the individual using them and his or her suitability to the problem at hand. Relevance tools make sense when they help refine customer targeting, specifically the who (potential value), the how (experience), and the what (point in time) of customer engagement.

The tools and the target come together in equation-based marketing. A company using equation-based marketing can design the mechanisms it needs to identify its most profitable shoppers, based on their value or purchasing behaviors, the best contextual environments and methods for reaching them, and which offers are most likely to inspire the desired response. Equation-based marketing is a step up from basic campaign measurement because it's systematic. Any campaign planner worth his qualitative salt can design a marketing campaign for a target demographic in the right seasonal period. Witness the entire back-to-school marketing bonanza as evidence. But can he build a series of successive campaigns over an extended period targeted at specific individuals based on each person's loyalty behaviors?

Equation-based marketing will help you determine which resources to invest in in order to keep your best customers satisfied, while also recognizing those underdeveloped customers who should get their fair share of communications, yet be messaged differently to improve their spending potential. It makes sense to target based on both the current and potential values of your customers. The first guarantees sustainable revenue; the second is your ticket to growth.

Next is the how of customer engagement, or how to create messages that resonate with target customers based on their current or potential worth. Equation-based algorithms manage a bank of offers and an optimization engine that matches the best offer to a target customer. They do this in two steps. First they rank the messages that merchants or business owners want to send on the basis of customer need. The messages themselves can be generic, such as announcing a sale this coming Saturday, but the algorithm will determine the likely target customer. Next, recognizing that nobody wants to be overwhelmed with unrequested messages, the algorithm employs a decision engine to define which of those messages is going to be most relevant to a select customer. Some customers sit up and take notice when you offer them preferential treatment, upgrades, or access to exclusive events. Others dream of aspirational rewards, such as a free weekend or destination package. And then there are the solid citizens who are watching their wallets; simply wanting offers that save dollars and cents.

Finally, the preferred message is selected based on where the customer is at a point in time, or what marketing messages will resonate. Consider the FedEx Game Time program, a multichannel campaign that targets customers at a point in time: during the NFL season, from September through December. In 2010 FedEx decided to kick engagement higher, with a more targeted approach using a customer value database and integrated Web platform powered by Epsilon. It customized the Game Time campaign for loyalty members, rewarding them for their business and reaching them through targeted, multichannel communications. FedEx reviews a number of specific criteria to determine which customers will best perform in the campaign. The strategy delivered considerable yardage—almost nineteen thousand customers signed up to participate in 2010, a 66 percent increase year-over-year.

Timing is a critical factor in customer choice, and if you can shorten the length of time between when an unmet need is identified, the message is designed, and the customer receives it, you significantly increase the odds of relevance. For instance, we know how many SMS texts are opened in the three hours after they're sent compared to the open-rate of e-mails. The knowledge provided through such tracking is making it increasingly possible to pinpoint messaging opportunities across different channels, by person and by time of day.

The four doors provide the contextual understanding of how to target groups of customers. Put more simply: While it is necessary to analyze the data in isolation, the four doors are a means of correlating the information intelligently, so you know which actions to take. The doors tell you that today's recent graduate will be tomorrow's futon shopper. A young professional may buy the same detergent as her grandmother, but one prefers to communicate via cell phone while the other through direct mail. The four doors tell us that an avid bowler may actually prefer to eat at the same restaurants as an opera fan.

Ignore the power of the doors at your peril. Without these insights your efforts to be relevant may turn out to be an annoyance, and that's a zero-gain game.

Door One: Spatial—It's Where You're At

The spatial door refers literally to a person's location. It finds the neighborhood the customer lives in, his or her daily travel routes, and the places where he or she does business. Because few industries can determine where the consumer is at all times, other than cell phone makers and those that can literally track a customer's location, most of us project likely movements based on a person's home and workplace. No one drives one hundred miles to get her hair cut, after all.

Spatial activity enables marketers to identify customers who are physically near their own businesses, so they can engage them in timely offers that would coincide with their daily routines.

And what can be more routine than eating? McDonald's in Finland, in partnership with Nokia mobile advertising subsidiary NAVTEQ, successfully used location-based marketing by delivering mobile ads to certain app users when they were near one of its eighty-two locations. Consumers who clicked on the mobile ads viewed a promotion—one cheeseburger for one euro—as well as driving or walking directions to the nearest location. Almost 40 percent of those consumers selected the click-to-navigate option, while the overall pilot program resulted in a click-through rate of 7 percent.[2]

McDonald's realized early on that the proliferation of digital properties provides us with specific visibility of the customer's location. But at the same time, these technologies provide the customer with a powerful comparison-shopping tool. Spatial analysis has taken on a whole new dimension with geolocation applications and social networks such as Foursquare, Gowalla, MyTown, and Loopt. And new companies looking to leverage this technology are popping up every quarter.[3]

But in its most basic form, spatial activity is about geography, and sometimes it illuminates unexpected patterns. Consider one of our clients, a tire and auto services chain that, in an effort to acquire new customers, geocoded which of its regular patrons lived within a close radius to its stores. It did this to define its marketing trade area by franchisee or dealer group. But when it analyzed how people shopped it found a limited correlation between their home addresses and the sites they used. Digging deeper, we then looked at other businesses these same shoppers frequented and were able to identify two "hot spots" where customers concentrated their activity: the workplace and home. There is nothing data analysts like better than a straightforward solution to a complex problem. The chain overlapped both geographic locations, and voilà, it discovered a high correlation between the centers of both activities.

But the chain couldn't predict if someone would prefer to have his car serviced close to home or close to work. So the company reverted to a marketwide strategy, acquiring customers across all of its area locations instead of in the simple geographical trade areas it originally used. In doing so it was able to target potential customers whether they serviced their vehicles close to home or close to work, and in the process, it maximized the value of the campaign.

Door Two: Temporal—The Big Events

The temporal door follows a similar pattern of analysis, this time to identify life events or a series of points in time that are indicative of present or future behavior. These events may also serve as a prompt for targeted messaging. Sticking with the automotive example, such capabilities would be programmed into my car, reminding me of my next service visit based on the automatic resetting of the clock every six months.

Temporal events are often indicative of bigger life changes, such as a new baby or a move to your first house. Years ago, when Sears was our client, its executives told me that their customers' potential value more than doubled after they secured their first mortgage.

But these events can also be less significant, such as home renovation projects or a family reunion. A vacation is an example of a temporal shift. If a credit card customer just purchased plane tickets to Hawaii, then you probably have a very short window of time to target offers for a hotel room, a rental car, or even surfing lessons. Or, to be even more immediate, a marketer could interest the traveler in trip insurance. The catch is to capture the consumer when he or she is most likely to be receptive to your offer.

This is where cell phone technology can be especially helpful. The increase in smartphone use—roughly 40 percent of the U.S. population in 2011—is giving rise to a completely new channel of communications based on point-in-time consumer activities.[4] Globally, more than two thirds of respondents to a 2011 survey said they used a smartphone for personal (73 percent) or business (69 percent) purposes.[5]

The potential is astounding. The consumer's ability to compare product prices across multiple retailers completely transforms the buying process and presents enormous opportunities for triggered messaging—those messages that respond to a consumer's recent activity. Imagine being able to identify a customer who is looking up restaurant reviews and then sending him an offer for a nearby restaurant with better ratings. Twitter and a host of other social media sites, including Facebook and Yelp!, open a world of review and/or bidding opportunities for consumers, many of whom have made a practice of asking everyone in their networks to weigh in on what to wear, where to dine, or which phone to buy.

As life-stage events go, new movers are the jackpot of consumer behavior changes, a phenomenon explored by Epsilon Targeting in its 2010 report by the same name. Its research showed that nearly 4.4 million people had relocated in the United States in the first four months of 2010, compared with about 3.9 million in the same period in 2009. This uptick translated into billions of dollars in retail purchases, based on moving.com data that showed new movers spent an average of $9,400 per household, a figure that was 29 percent higher than it was in 2007. While many of those purchases included bubble wrap, boxes, and moving vans, roughly $1,200 of that $9,400 was discretionary, earmarked specifically for home décor and other nonmoving items.

Additionally, the research determined that new movers spent the bulk of their relocation money in the quarter in which they moved, after which spending trailed off over twelve months. In some categories, such as home décor, spending dropped even faster. There was also a temporal aspect to the map of the purchasing sequence—tools and electronic sales climbed 23 percent right after a move, then dropped to 15 percent several quarters later. Likewise, spending in the apparel, gift, business-to-business, and senior categories declined early in the move and resumed six months after.[6]

Temporal promotions are not a new phenomenon, with January gym memberships and February chocolates being the stock example. But what differs in the four doors is that such analysis tracks the customer's value today and in the future. MasterCard identifies Tuesdays and Wednesdays as the biggest shopping days for online apparel, meaning these are good days to promote similar services, since the customer is more likely to be in shopping mode already. Unlike fliers stuffed randomly in the mailbox, the customer message in these cases is tailored to reflect time, place, and value. If you knew, for instance, that I routinely quit my gym membership in March, you might conclude that that's the month to engage me in a health plan.

Door Three: Individual—It's All About You

But regardless of where a person is in life, whether it's work, vacation, or the mall, his or her personal preferences shape almost all purchase decisions. This is where it gets personal and the "individual" door opens. It is sensitive territory, because we've crossed the threshold into a consumer's passions and values, from motorcycle riding to composting. Remember my story earlier on about the NBAStore.com? The NBAStore.com failed to register my preferred team, even though it did recognize that I am a basketball fan.

All of those advanced-class algorithms and real-time tracking come to bear in sifting through the individual tastes, values, and needs of consumers. They establish the difference between knowing a shopper buys her shoes online and that she buys her shoes only at a discount from DSW.com. And they can help to distinguish what types of products a person may purchase. A high-end consumer may buy her detergent and batteries at Walmart—meaning it can capture her spatially and temporally—but it is not likely to get her to buy its George line of clothing, because she prefers luxury apparel.

Further, by cross-referencing a customer's online viewing and shopping behavior, a marketer can determine her age and gender and ensure its marketing images and tone are agreeable.

Identifying unmet needs is the most challenging exercise of all, but individual preferences can be applied successfully at the storewide level. In a classic example of a customer-committed organization, Best Buy launched a well-known test in which it segmented its favored shoppers, and then sent targeted offers for products and services to encourage them to spend more and return often.[7] Relying on a complex database analysis that partnered purchase information with demographics—including personal interests and product preferences—Best Buy was able to identify four specific types of customers in its stores, and it then went on to determine which stores should cater to each type of customer.

The "Barry" shopper, for instance, is an affluent professional who demands top-shelf technology and service. "Jill," meanwhile, is a suburban mother interested in providing her kids with technology and entertainment. "Ray" is a price-conscious family man who wants technology to improve his daily life. And "Buzz" is the young, active male, possibly a techie, who wants the latest technology and entertainment. There is also a fifth segment, the SB, which stands for the small business customer.

With this knowledge in hand Best Buy redesigned stores to ensure that each of these customer groups could navigate the store and treat it as a destination. Further, it trained its employees to look for Barry, Jill, Ray, and Buzz, so they could serve them better. Sales rose to $50.3 billion in fiscal 2011 from almost $30.9 billion in fiscal 2006.[8] In the same period its biggest competitor, Circuit City, went out of business.

Door Four: Cultural/Cohorts—Who's Your Buddy?

The final door leads to the cultural definitions of consumers. You may even refer to it as the cohort door, since oftentimes the people who we want to hang out with define our "culture." And by culture I do mean the standard definition of race, religion, and even sexual orientation. But it also includes any committed action or lifestyle choice that defines a person's activities, from triathletes to churchgoers to avid sports fans.

The National Hockey League, for instance, knows that more than half of its fans live outside the city of their favorite team, meaning the characteristics that unite them as a culture are not necessarily geographical. The NHL does not operate an actual loyalty program, but it does know that most of its twenty million avid fans are exceptionally tech savvy—another characteristic of the culture. So it reaches out to these fans from well beyond the rink and across all digital channels, from television to the computer and from the tablet to the cell phone. Wherever its fans are, the NHL goes with them. It has learned a great deal about content favorites along the way, such as which videos are most likely to go viral and the best monetization prospects in social media.[9]

Cultural groups are easy to identify as a rule, because inclusion is a big part of how a person defines himself or herself. They are a united entity moving through a common experience. For this reason a person's culture is shorthand for the context they should be marketed within. Just as you would speak a different language to cricket versus hockey fans, you would engage members of a Chinese community in different ways than you would those of a Jewish community.

Take an innocuous example, like grape juice. In 2005, professors at the Stanford Graduate School of Business and the University of Sydney performed a study to explore cultural influences on consumer behavior.[10] They asked Anglo and Asian American students to view advertisements for Welch's grape juice, and then randomly assigned them into two groups. They instructed one segment to provide their immediate reactions to the spots, while the others were advised to spend some time thinking about the ads' effectiveness.

Half of the ads touted the benefits that could be gained by drinking the grape juice, such as higher energy levels, good taste, and pleasure. The other ads focused on the juice's preventive advantages, including its health benefits and ability to reduce the risk of some cancers and heart disease.

In their immediate reactions to the ads, the Asian American students indexed heavily toward the preventive messages, while the Anglo American students preferred the promotional ones. According to a report on the research, in the *Stanford GSB News:* "This tallied with the researchers' theories that Americans, who value achievement, accomplishment, and independent thinking, would focus on the positive consequences of their purchasing decisions. On the other hand, Chinese subjects, who tend to value protection and security, and have more interdependent ways of viewing the world, were expected to concentrate on the negative consequences of their actions or decisions."

What the researchers might not have expected, however, was that those remaining students who were asked to think and reflect on the ads showed no significant differences in which ad they preferred, whether they were Anglo Americans or Asian Americans. While these results might not benefit long-term marketing campaigns, they can be applied spatially. In Asian communities, for instance, a grocer would position its in-store promotions for juice around preventive messages. Since most purchase decisions are made in the aisle, the odds of connecting with that customer are higher.

What If I Go Through a Door and No One's Home?

It goes without saying that no consumer should be pigeonholed behind one door. It is for this reason that data is so essential in aligning the framework of the four doors. Regardless of the door you find yourself entering, remember that what is on the other side does not exist in a vacuum. It is common sense that the insights beyond each of these doors will shift and change throughout the consumer's life. But they each provide the practical context needed to talk to customers today, and to plan for tomorrow. Without this filter, a consumer could be missed by a minute or a mile. Reaching out to a young mother with a diaper message when she just finished toilet training her toddler is ineffectual. Sending credit card offers to a client who just lost his house is too risky.

So what do we need to do differently to go through the four doors? Well, forgive me for banging the data drum again, but it starts with a leap into customer information. If you treat customer data points in a one-dimensional fashion, you have no choice but to be a reactive marketer: I know you own a cat; I'll send you a cat food offer. I know you bought a house; I'll send you a mortgage offer. In order to build customer intimacy, companies have no choice but to embrace the complexity of multidimensional data, and this could involve some heavy statistical lifting. So start warming up, because the greater value comes when the marketer recognizes that collecting customer data is a cumulative exercise, growing richer as more elements are added and behavior is tracked over time.

Digital retailers have it easier, because they can track online behaviors, and Amazon.com is still the master at storytelling. The world's largest online retailer registers not just your individual purchases, but also your searches, and then it suggests related products based on that activity. Further, it will recommend products that were purchased by other consumers who have searched for and bought similar products. And Amazon.com will post reviews written by purchasers of the products you are researching. In effect, Amazon.com works as a personal shopper. I only wish it would insert a simple check box to mark whether the purchase is a gift. That way it could avoid sending me a series of music recommendations stemming from a gift I regret purchasing last Christmas.

The point is that there are few companies that are capturing and effectively using the wealth of information behind all four doors, but there are many that are using some of it very well. Likewise, don't expect to be able to do it all at once, especially at the start. The crawl-walk-run approach is often best, because it prevents major missteps that can cost your customer's trust. It's not marketing voodoo; just a step up from the recency, frequency, monetary (RFM) analyses that direct marketers have used for decades to identify the best prospects for targeted communications. And as with RFM marketing, a basic level of logic applies. At a minimum, you should be thinking: Who do I want to target? What experiences do I want to create? And at what point in time do I want to engage in communications?

Don't Overthink This

In fact, logic is essential every step of the way if we ever want to keep pace with customer needs and win their loyalty. If we are ever to reach those 68 percent of consumers who say their loyalty communications are irrelevant, and to get them to say "Yes! Loyalty-based marketing is resonating with me and hitting all the right notes of relevance!" then we all need to be combining elements of the four doors in keeping with the consumer's evolving lifestyle.

There are technical and tactical requirements to getting there in addition to the collection and management of data across multiple dimensions. Even when the loyalty strategy is right and the company is connecting with the consumer one-on-one, driving significance all the way through to the customer-committed side of the interaction, you may still want to invest differently in technology. Remember, even at the point of emotional loyalty, the consumer may experience significant life changes that can put your relationship at risk, or at least alter its significance. When a consumer moves, for example, location-based services are a jump ball, to use a basketball metaphor. Where that customer fills up for gas, buys groceries, or gets his clothes cleaned are all affected by where he lives. You need to maintain the entire equation-based structure, keeping the algorithms, offer optimization, and real-time tracking humming in the background. And let's not forget that your best customers expect more, so forgetting their favorite team or their birthday could be quite the letdown.

The really neat part in all of this is that this valued customer is choosing to share all of her behavioral information with *you*—expressly so you can enhance her experience. At any given time there are levers you can pull to activate engagement, from location to life events and culture to causes.

There is no doubt that getting through the four doors takes a lot of work, but it is a small investment to make to achieve emotional loyalty and customer intimacy. In fact, the outcome has the potential to be so precious that some would say it requires a good dose of hope.

CHAPTER 6

Turning Fear on Its Ear: Can You Inspire Loyalty Through Hope?

Back in high school, when my leading preoccupations included soccer games and biology classes, and long before I turned my sights to a lifetime in loyalty and customer intimacy, I spent my days with my face turned toward the sun.

I was not alone. Throughout the summers of the 1970s and 1980s millions of people from across the globe ventured out to the beach, the poolside, the park, or the rooftop in pursuit of a deep, dark tan. All sorts of methods were tested to intensify our bronzing: foil-lined reflectors, baby oil, and even butter were pulled from closets and refrigerators. And for those who worked all day, sunlamps were plugged into the bedroom. Coppertone ran full-color magazine advertisements featuring swimsuit models the approximate color of roast turkeys, alongside the message: YOU OWN THE SUN WITH COPPERTONE.

It was universally understood: Beautiful people were tan.

These days, the start of summer—May—is designated as Skin

Cancer Awareness month. More than sixty-eight thousand new cases of lethal melanoma were diagnosed in the United States in 2010, with eighty-seven hundred deaths, according to the National Cancer Institute. The prognosis is that one in five Americans will eventually develop some form of skin cancer.[1]

The disease does not recognize socioeconomic, cultural, or social barriers, let alone beauty. Among public figures who have fought skin cancer are former U.S. presidential candidate John McCain, who was treated for a recurrence of melanoma in 2000. The late Elizabeth Taylor in 2003 was treated for basal cell carcinoma. Talk and game show host Regis Philbin was diagnosed with skin cancer twice, once after having a small growth excised by a doctor during the airing of his popular morning show. And actress Melanie Griffith underwent surgery to have early stage skin cancer removed in 2009.[2]

Not surprisingly, the makers of skin-care products were soon recruiting celebrities to endorse skin cancer awareness and pledge sun celibacy. By 2008, the actress Marcia Cross of *Desperate Housewives* was in her second year of a campaign with the American Society for Dermatologic Surgery and the skincare brand Olay, made by Procter & Gamble Co. Actress Kristen Bell, meanwhile, campaigned with Jergens, a P&G competitor, to benefit the Skin Cancer Foundation.[3] And in 2011, celebrities including Brandy, Tatyana Ali, and Danielle Fishel posed naked, though not fully exposed, in public service announcements about the dangers of going outdoors without sunscreen.[4]

The thing is, many of the sun-protective products populating the aisles by this time were not actual sunscreens. Rather, makers of everything from facial moisturizers to lip balm to cosmetics were including sunscreen in their brands as a product *enhance-*

ment that pledged not only to fight cancer but to stop aging. Based on the amount of sunscreen protection out there, you'd think the sun's rays were deadly on contact. And if they didn't kill you, they'd immediately make you look ten years older.

But it was a boom business. Noncosmetic sunscreen product sales rose to almost $800 million by 2009, despite a recession that kept many people from summer travel.[5] That was up from about $500 million in 2006, according to the *New York Times*.[6]

Long gone are those eight-hour days at the poolside when tan lines were seductive and sun-kissed skin was a sign of healthy living. Nowadays tanned skin gives off a precancerous glow.

Such awareness has definitely benefited the populace, since it has likely prevented many cases of cancer, but it also elevated sun protection from a health aid to a beauty aid. The fear of skin damage is so widespread, and access to prevention so seemingly easy, that there is little argument against spending slightly more for the protection, however limited.

In 2011, the swell of product innovations caused the Food and Drug Administration to announce new regulations for sunscreen labeling, to take effect in 2012. Among them, it is prohibiting any company from calling sunscreen "sunblock" or from labeling it as waterproof, since that is basically impossible.[7]

The sunscreen industry was founded on a real fear. But its multiproduct expansion, to everything from facial wash to shampoos, is marketed on the same trepidations, because whether it is real or exaggerated, fear sells. It always has. Fear is what moves insurance policies, weight loss systems, and Rogaine. It is why women will spend more for an antiwrinkle cream if it has microbeads, and why Viagra sales are almost $2 billion globally.[8] Fear convinces people to invest in GPS systems for their cars and cell phones for their teenagers. The marketing message behind all of these products is the same: If you don't buy it, something bad will happen. You'll get fat. You'll go bald. You won't perform. No one will love you. Your family will be left homeless and penniless. You'll be an outcast.

Entire industries thrive on fear. Sales of antibacterial products in the United States, including hand wipes and gels such as Purell, exceeded $1 billion in 2010,[9] thanks largely to concerns about SARS and the H1N1 virus. Australian pillow maker Tontine in 2011 introduced "freshness date stamps" to encourage people to replace their synthetic pillows every two years to prevent dust mites, sweat stains, and other frightful things. Sales of the newly stamped pillows in the first week of its fresh-pillow campaign rose 345 percent.[10] And the bedbug infestation that struck in 2007 resulted in a multifold growth in bedbug extermination sales, which advanced to $258 million in 2009 from $98 million 2006, according to the National Pest Management Association.[11] Some exterminators launched entire bedbug divisions, going so far as to purchase and train bedbug-sniffing dogs.

Fear has proven equally effective in getting people to stop certain habits, such as smoking, and to *not* stop doing certain things, such as wearing a seat belt. How often have you been warned that if you no longer visit a specific store you'll miss its supersales and great offers?

Our own marketing results validate what most marketers already know: Fear not only sells, but it sells differently based on the consumer segment and life stage. For example, one of our surveys reveals that younger consumers are more likely to adhere to their drug prescription regimes if they are warned that missing it could lead to illness, which in turn would lead to missed work and possibly becoming a burden to one's family. People who are older than fifty-five, however, are more motivated by price, which may speak to the fear of having to choose between medication and food.

Which brings me to a loyalty-related question: If fear is effective for selling products, is it also useful to building loyalty? It may be, depending on your approach. The challenge is in packaging the message of fear while still leaving the customer with a positive connection toward your brand. I'd call that the advanced class of brand management, and I warn you, it could be a tall task when the goal is long-term customer intimacy. But there is a healthy way around it. I propose we look at fear in the inverse, which is to say, we should market on the message of hope.

Let's explore our basic fears for a moment and the corresponding hopes that can be derived from each.

Fear of Commitment? Nahhhh . . .

Although fear of sun damage, or even of lipstick sticking to your teeth, probably won't make the Top Ten list of phobias, it's fair to say that our most minor fears are only one or two steps removed from a deeply rooted concern most people share. They each reach the consumer on a very personal level, addressing fundamental fears we all have—loss of a child, getting sick, becoming unattractive to those we love, abandonment.

Many of our fears actually target the basic instincts of survival.

Psychologists identify five very basic fears that motivate most of our actions, and when used by marketers they can influence and determine the products we buy. These five fears are:

- **death:** Perhaps our most visceral fear is loss—of our family members, our friends, others in our tight social circle, and ourselves. Lots of medications and medical processes are sold on the back of this fear, not to mention precautionary products like bike helmets and, of course, those little kits that will help you break out of your car the next time it is submerged in water.

- **strangers:** Outsiders may attack us, steal our jobs, or force us to do something we do not want to do. The makers of home alarm systems have been very effective in dialing up the scare factor here, with TV ads that show a menacing masked man targeting the home of a young woman who is clearly alone.
- **the unknown:** While we all enjoy a little spontaneity now and then, we take a lot of comfort in believing we have the power to manage our future. This is the reason we tend to fall into routines. It is also why AAA memberships, retirement plans, and life insurance policies are so popular.
- **chaos:** Humans crave order. We sleep best knowing we have some measure of control over almost everything, from international terror threats to the dust on our shelves. Our tendency toward order is what persuades us to buy cleaning products, guns, and generators.
- **insignificance:** Perhaps the most marketable fear, the one of insignificance taps into our insecurities of not making an impact on society, or of not being loved or accepted. A gamut of products, from hair thickener to toning shoes to Victoria's Secret push-up bras, are sold based on the fear of insignificance.

I propose that almost every form of human interaction can potentially scare up one of these fears in some way. Say someone takes your work project away: What fears are conjured up by this action? You may feel rejected, or become concerned that you are not getting the recognition you deserve. You might worry that your job suddenly seems unnecessary, and that you will be fired and lose your house. And you might even fear the qualifications of this unknown worker—will he screw this up?

In a similar fashion, almost every form of business interaction can awaken one of these fears. When the customer chooses to try cell phone banking for the first time, he'll likely have many fears—two out of five U.S. consumers believed cell phone banking was unsafe as recently as 2011, while ownership of smartphones increased to 34 percent from 15 percent between 2009 and 2011.[12] So a new cell phone banking customer would undoubtedly wonder: Is my information safe? What if a stranger hacks into the account and steals my money? Can my identity be stolen, creating chaos for my family? Is my personal information going to be sold to a bunch of marketers who will inundate me with spam?

These privacy concerns are very real and should be recognized as a fundamental business matter for any company that collects and uses data, much like pricing strategies and merchandise selections are day-to-day issues a company faces. You simply cannot ignore the instinctive concerns people have about releasing confidential information; it taps into some of the base fears people have regarding chaos and the unknown, the inability to know the future. It's simply a matter of self-preservation.

Whether you run a loyalty program or are simply collecting customer information for marketing purposes, you need to be aware of the real fears that consumers have about companies collecting and using their personal information. That said, we're pretty fortunate that loyalty programs, although they are instruments for collecting data, can also serve to calm these fears. Through regular communications, a loyalty program has the opportunity to keep its members apprised of how it is using their personal data and why, offering a level of transparency and confidence in its business practices. This clarity reduces the fear of chaos and translates to a stronger sense of law and order, while the issuance of rewards and other forms of recognition reinforces the members' feelings of significance. Finally, through the right use of engagement activities, loyalty programs serve as broader communities, where each member is welcome among like-minded people—not strangers.

Are Scare Tactics Good for Building Customer Relationships?

As I mentioned earlier, fear is a potent marketing tool, but unless it delivers a positive association with your brand it will not guarantee loyalty. Loyalty is the result of customer intimacy, not terror. However, if you turn these fears on their collective ear, they serve as healthy motivators, because fear operates at a deeper emotional level. Fears can inspire us to do social work, connect with family, live healthier. For marketers they open up message receptors, allowing us to connect with the consumer. Indeed, the underlying hopes summoned by these five basic fears aim at the heart of loyalty and why loyalty should work.

Which is to say, if you are going to become customer-committed, then you have to shape your product and message around your customers' belief systems and ambitions. What this all points to, of course, is that big R: relevance.

Striking Relevance into the Hearts of Consumers

By now you know my stand on the importance of relevance for building long-term loyalty and profitable customer relationships. Now let's venture deeper into its anatomy to see how it produces the lifeblood of company-customer collaborations.

Much like the arteries of the human heart are divided, forming the vessels of our daily existence, relevance also bifurcates into two types, each of which helps to transport our message to consumers. To understand them, we'll want to recall the four doors: spatial, temporal, individual, and cultural (STIC).

The first type of relevance is in the "deliberate context," and it encompasses many of the consumer characteristics behind the spatial and temporal doors, including one's physical location, special occasions, and life stages. Relevance in the deliberate context typically relies on rewards and offers, since it is triggered by an event or is targeted regionally. A dog owner may jump at an offer for a half-price grooming, but not if the Bow-Wow Boutique is thirty miles away. Because of its promotional basis, tactical relevance tends to arouse behavioral loyalty among consumers.

The second form of relevance exists in the "context of resonance," and it responds to those consumer qualities behind the individual and cultural doors, such as passions, values, and ethnicities. Relevance in the resonant context says "I know who you are." It creates value around a consumer's core underlying interests, leading to emotional loyalty and engagement. That, in turn, builds brand value and customer equity.

The type of relevance you strive for will determine the level of your customer's behavioral or emotional loyalty. And while emotional loyalty is the backbone of intimacy, you do want a mix. After all, you need to be where your customers are and to keep pace with the events in their lives in order for them to know that you care. You don't have to be forceful about it; few consumers would welcome an offer for a dating service one month after a spouse dies. But an offer for a gym membership, painting classes, or a cruise could strike a more meaningful chord.

The point is to be deft, and responsible, with the data you collect. There are overt ways of marketing a product or service (keeps babies drier) and then there are covert methods for reinforcing your underlying message (your baby's health depends on you). The execution of this covert, or stealth, marketing harkens back to the rules regarding content and context. Any successful motivational communication needs first to include the proper content and then to be positioned within the appropriate context, not only to influence consumer behavior but also to obtain loyalty. Both are critical elements of this mix and a requirement for striking the appropriate balance of the right message at the right time.

The Brands that Fear (and Hope) Built

But what does relevance have to do with fear and hope? Well, a relevant message really begins with a brand and the type of relationship it chooses to build with its customers. Michael Silverstein and Neil Fiske, in their book *Trading Up*, outline a simple model for scaling the peak to genuine differentiation among consumers. The toeholds of this peak help to define the customer experience on three levels: technical, functional, and emotional.[13]

Let's look at these levels at play. Toyota doesn't use bikinis and hard rock to sell its cars; its brand is built on reliability and safety. CapitalOne doesn't position itself as a credit card for the wealthy or million-mile members; it's a rule-breaking card for consumers who worry about high interest rates, penalty fees, and a lot of requirements.

Even brands that are not actual products can produce a message that, relevancywise, strikes a perfect pitch. Have you been to Las Vegas lately? The city has established itself not merely as a tourist destination but as a getaway from the shackles and demands of everyday life. Its slogan—"What Happens Here, Stays Here"—is a brand marketer's dream. The catchphrase is expansive enough to capture the imagination of every visitor from college students to retirees, but it also hits a deep emotional chord. Every one of us has something we would occasionally like to spirit ourselves away from—children, work, cleaning, yard work, or even the constant hum of a routine, safe as it is. The tagline, developed in 1999 by R&R Partners for the Las Vegas Convention and Visitors Authority, may not awaken any resonant notes of fear, but it does awaken hope—to be adventurous, to try new things, and to possibly be a winner, earning respect and admiration among one's peers.

Most brands, like these, differentiate themselves on three levels. First they stand apart on a technical level. Their workmanship, technology, and materials distinguish the product from others in the same competitive space. Chipotle Mexican Grill separates itself from other quick-serve chains by using ingredients that are raised locally and humanely, a practice it calls "food with integrity." This marketing message serves a second purpose of eliminating worries about eating unhealthy food.

These technical distinctions should lead to the next step, which is functional performance. The product should deliver results in a way that is wholly different from its competitors. The economy class offerings on Singapore Airlines, including Givenchy fleece blankets, personal LCD screens, and ergonomically designed seats, consistently assure its ranking among best-performing airlines.

Combined, these features should engage the customer emotionally and on a memorable level, through the singular experience that the brand delivers.

These levels of differentiation determine, for example, how a hotel is laid out, the feel of the rooms, and the features or amenities within. Think about it. A Holiday Inn Express provides house-branded bars of soap, while the Ritz-Carlton offers Bulgari products. Just that one technical element is a key part of delivering the desired experience.

But none of these differentiators will, on its own, fulfill the ultimate goal, which is emotional engagement. The real point of differentiation comes when those discriminating product features (shampoos, linens, the desk clerk) are presented in a way that engages the customer emotionally. Which is to say that they should all function to answer to the needs of the desired customer.

Let's carry the hotel example through to the experiential level. If I'm in a Holiday Inn Express, the expectation is for an inexpensive and functional experience. I am there because I am on a budget and looking for a fast and easy trip, complete with parking. I know what to expect—there is no fear of the unknown, no worries about going over budget. But if I am in a Ritz-Carlton I am looking for leisure, perhaps an impressive setting for a breakfast meeting, or more indulgent evenings. Basically, I am searching for an emotionally different experience but still have an idea of what to expect.

The way you create a completely unique brand experience is by stacking the deck. In other words, the company decides upon the encounter it wants to create for the customer, and then it recognizes the functional characteristics necessary to deliver that experience. It's then up to the company to reverse engineer the technical features of the product or service so that it can make good on the promise.

Let's see how these qualities apply to products that can be purchased and brought home. Let's say that down the street from the hotel is a lululemon athletica store. This specialty chain, which sells privately branded men's and women's yoga and athletic apparel, specializes in fabrics and materials that are state of the art, attractive, and of the highest comfort. The designs are functional but chic, and they can be worn from the gym to happy hour. Further, in addition to being comfortable and stylish, lululemon apparel serves the purpose of being very effective for workouts. There's no stink, no chafing. The seams are in all the right places, so there is no discomfort as you twist into various yoga positions. Such qualities speak to the lifestyle needs of its customers.

These are powerful distinguishing features. But what connects customers to lululemon as a brand is that it makes people feel they are part of a broader community that thrives on wellness and better living. It markets on hope. This emotional aspect is taken to the experiential level within the store environment: the look of the displays; the physical fitness of the employees; their product knowledge; and the regularly updated inventory that speaks to lululemon's dedication to being current and fashionable.

Lululemon's performance with consumers is reflected on its income statement. Its sales per square foot exceeded $1,700 in 2010, translating to annual sales of more than $711 million, up from $453 million in 2009, while net income advanced to $122 million from $58 million in the same period.[14]

All brands, big, small, and basic, are composed of technical and functional components. And all of their elements guide the customer's definition of the brand experience and how he or she frames and remembers that experience. This process arcs back to emotional loyalty. And remember, I am not writing about loyalty programs but about true customer loyalty and how that customer values your brand.

We Fear, Therefore We Hope

Once you do reach emotional engagement through the brand, you expose yourself to the same sentiments that prompt so many of our actions, including our purchase decisions: fear and hope.

I wish I could put hope first, but the unfortunate truth is that, of the two, fear is typically the bigger motivator. Fear causes people to change their behaviors to avoid a bad outcome. We know that fear sells billions of dollars in products every year, from antivirus software to mascara to duct tape. Fear will always be a powerful motivator, and it can be used to influence many positive outcomes. But it does not necessarily build loyalty.

By turning fear into hope companies can create real value among their customer base. Let's look at the five fears when they are turned into hope:

Death of Self or Clan →	Defense and Security
Stranger(s) →	Bonding and Community
Unknown/Future →	Understanding and Clarity
Chaos →	Law and Order
Insignificance →	Recognition and Impact

These fears even link back to some of the underpinnings of loyalty program development. Many companies own warehouses of customer data but might not recognize the needs and concerns of these same customers, some of whom are worried about how that information is being collected and used.

But an examination of the opposite of each of these fears reveals pure hope. Worried that bacon is too fatty? Well, blueberries are rich in antioxidants. Is sleepiness making you dull-witted? Red Bull gives you wings. Does dust threaten to make you look like a lazy mother? Swiffer makes cleaning a breeze.

Fear is the reason why we have air bags, vaccines, and diapers. But it also is why PUR water filters are saving millions of lives in third-world countries today.

Death? Give Us Life, Wellness, Security

What can be more hopeful than a flower? The cheerful echinacea plant has for years been considered a holistic protector against colds and other illnesses. Sales of echinacea products totaled about $155 million in 2007.[15] This despite repeated medical studies that have concluded that the herb is ineffective.

Hope inspires us to make many healthy and sustainable lifestyle choices—for ourselves, for the planet, and for others. A 2011 study by research-services provider Ipsos for Procter & Gamble revealed that 70 percent of women said they would like to back causes through everyday purchases, while 53 percent said they think companies should do more to encourage consumers to help support charitable causes. They also thought companies should make donating simpler.[16] And we agree. In 2010 LoyaltyOne introduced a new loyalty program called Air Miles for Social Change (AMSC).

Designed to benefit individuals, the community, and the earth, AMSC rewards members for making healthier, greener choices in their everyday lives, from the proper disposal of batteries to carpooling. Roughly three hundred thousand of our AIR MILES members engaged in the AMSC programs in its first year, and the number is growing. Canadian transit pass sales advanced by 57 percent through the AMSC program. It has helped to increase e-billing conversions by 72 percent and boosted participation in a power-saving campaign by a remarkable 700 percent.

The motivation for such improvements, from the individual to the earth, is based in hope. We all want to feel better, and we want to make the earth a better place for our children. An undercurrent of fear, such as animal extinction and global warming, directs these same actions, but a positive message is still steering the movement. Save the polar bears!

Strangers? We Like Bonding with Family, Friends, and Communities

From pottery classes to happy hours, many social events are marketed on the basis of making friends, strengthening bonds, and expanding your social circle. But when it comes to breaking the barriers between strangers and us, few have been as effective as the tourism industry. Nations from New Zealand to India have been lauded for their "you're welcome here" promotional campaigns. And the international travel guru Rick Steves, known for his *Europe Through the Back Door* guidebooks, has generated legions of dedicated followers through his publications, PBS series, and radio programs, all of which encourage us to get out there and get to know our foreign neighbors.

And sometimes these hopeful marketing messages promise love. In 2007 the online dating service Match.com launched a campaign in the United Kingdom that shifted its focus from women to men, with a message of hope that was hard to argue with. Called Too Many Women, the offer included one week of free membership, plus a "make love happen guarantee" that promised members that if they didn't find love in six months they would get an additional six months free. Notice Match.com's stealthy inclusion of the words "promise," "love," and "too many women"? In 2011 Match .com counted more than 4.6 million members in the UK alone.[17]

Unknown? We'll Go for Clarity Any Day

Breyers Ice Cream built its reputation on the purity of its product. Its slogan "Taste, not technology" sold a lot of gallons of rocky road, and it established the brand in the minds of many consumers as honest, reliable, and simple. The transparency of its ingredients put to rest emerging fears that we are feeding ourselves, and our children, preservatives and other ingredients that could cause cancer or worse.

The same kind of demystification benefits banks, marketers, and other companies that send their customers easy-to-understand privacy policies. The president of Nordstrom Bank in 2011 sent its credit-card holders personalized one-page, easy-to-read privacy notices that addressed the why, what, and how of its information collection practices, as well as a chart that explained the reasons it would share information and what information it does share and what it doesn't. In five minutes the card member felt like she was in secure hands.

Chaos? We Prefer Control, Law, and Order

When the U.S. Navy Seals assassinated Osama bin Laden in May 2011, it triggered an immediate international interest in these elite, highly specialized soldiers. But the military's real shortage of talent existed in its officer ranks. Two years earlier, in 2009, the U.S. Army had for the first time in its history launched a campaign to recruit them. Though similar to ads geared toward young rank-and-file recruits, complete with weapons and patriotic music, these spots were refined to appeal to college graduates who could qualify for one of the military's officer training programs. The TV spots featured images of such heroes as George Washington and Douglas MacArthur, underscoring the intended message that even the most goal-oriented graduates can aspire to a career in the army and help keep their country safe.[18]

On a more basic, everyday level, our homes are portrayed as battlefields, and a slew of problem-solving products, including lawn care, instant shower cleaners, and cat litter promise to easily keep our homes in order, despite the continued threat of chaos.

Insignificance? We'll Give You Recognition, Acceptance, and Love

At home and away, we all want to be needed, and an entire phenomenon—social networking—is built on the foundation of such recognition. People can check in to locations to mark their territory, maybe even become the mayors of their favorite coffee shops. By "liking" a business or comment on Facebook, we have the chance to make our opinions matter. When we have the opportunity to tweet a professional football player or famous comedian—

perchance to get a response—we tap into the hope of being recognized by a role model or idol. A proliferation of blogs covering everything from fashion to cars to small towns provides countless numbers of people the occasion to promote their opinions—and to get feedback.

I toast these efforts, and so does Maker's Mark, the distiller of Kentucky bourbon. Maker's Mark rewards those who share their good experiences about the bourbon by offering them the opportunity to become ambassadors. Maker's Mark makes excellent use of soft benefits, or experience-based recognition, to win its members. These soft benefits include: the member's name on a barrel of bourbon; advance notice of rare, special-release bottles; and a chance to purchase ambassador-only merchandise, including a bottle of bourbon from the ambassador's barrel. As a plus, members receive business cards with their name and title as "brand ambassador."

But really, any kind of social activity that makes people feel needed is founded in hope. The Peace Corps, the National Marrow Donor Program, food banks—they are all hope-based entities. Involvement in them makes for a better world, which validates your purpose, and you feel better about yourself.

We Hope, Therefore We Have Perspective

When thinking about what makes us tick, it is clear that relevance feeds the five hopes, and that loyalty can be a mechanism for delivering it. Consider it from a loyalty program perspective: When a marketer leads with clarity and an explicit articulation of the program's value to the customer, it provides the transparency to overcome fear of chaos and the unknown. Customers understand that they have the power to opt out of sharing their information, which gives them control of the exchange. And when done right, a program recognizes its customers for who they are and their commitment to the brand, thereby providing them with meaningful rewards that ensure an emotional connection, or friendship.

Through purposeful interactions, the consumer rises above this fear of insignificance and is motivated by the prospect of being recognized for her investment in the company, which becomes an investment in a cause. Not a cause such as cancer research or recycling, though those are powerful tools of hope, but the cause of supporting this company. The customer is so passionate about what it does that she'd run a mile for its success. Loyalty programs are instruments to engage the consumer. They feed our hopes.

So it's time for me to state my case for loyalty programs. Not as an overabundance of points and promotions, but loyalty programs as a means by which companies establish a deep emotional bond with people, its customers. Loyalty programs, when they form emotional bonds, create a community of sorts. Their members are not just individuals; they are bound by a common purpose. They know they are terrific customers, because they give the company more of their business and the company tells them it appreciates that. This recognition is valid and important, because they value all that the company does. It aligns with their purpose.

Fear does not go away, but it does mark the place where trust should enter the picture. Trust that we will safeguard the consumer's data versus the fear that we won't. Trust that we will always recognize the customer's loyalty, counting all her transactions toward points and ensuring that they will retain value, versus the fear that we will suddenly change the intrinsic value of these earned rewards.

Fear and hope even play a role in the Loyalty Leap, aiding the transition that enables the product obsessed and operational opportunists to become customer committed, simply by changing the perspective through which they consider their decisions. The real value in the shift is actually bringing this emotional component, this contextual environment, into the thinking process behind how the company delivers on everything it does. It is adding a level of richness to how the company envisions its brand and its interactions with the consumer.

Which is a school of thought that, in order to be effective, must be embraced companywide, from the corner office to the aisles. Such an approach is what separates the companies that have long-term, emotional partnerships with their customers from those that have tenuous relationships built on promotions and fear.

It is what delivers us to enterprise loyalty—an operational philosophy to which we all should aspire.

CHAPTER 7

Enterprise Loyalty: What Defines the Customer Experience?

If there is any fear that the company's loyalty marketing efforts aren't working, let me share a story that I like to call "coconuts to calling cards."

It was a few years back. Several of us were sitting in a conference room at LoyaltyOne headquarters discussing the ability of certain products to reveal the other purchases a consumer might make. In other words, if a shopper bought hot sauce, what other products would likely make their way into his or her basket? What did that specific product reveal about the shopper's lifestyle and needs?

It's the old potato-chips-and-dip theory. Or, as legend has it, beer and diapers. Many in the retail and consumer packaged goods industries have long believed there is a direct correlation between the purchase of diapers and that of beer, based on the speculation that if a man goes out to buy diapers, he'll likely think, "Well, it's almost the weekend, so I might as well grab a six-pack while I am here."

Coconuts to Calling Cards: Our "Beer-and-Diapers" Moment

At LoyaltyOne we possess an advanced technology that allows merchants to analyze their sales information at a customer level. We wanted to test the platform. So there we were, with members of the R&D team, tossing about high-minded hypotheses to gauge the power of the tool. "Give us any product and we'll run it," someone from the team challenged, and so, in a Monty Python moment, I blurted out the first word that came to mind: "Coconuts!"

The team right there and then ran the word "coconuts" through the relational database. Guess what was the third-highest product that correlated with coconuts? Prepaid calling cards, and yes, we were surprised too. Turns out that many consumers who buy coconuts emigrate from other parts of the world. And since coconuts are a staple of their native diet, the tropical food makes them homesick. So they buy calling cards.

It makes perfect sense, but I'm not sure we would have gotten there through any rational exercise. And that's my point. Consumers are not rational. They're sometimes quirky, sometimes erratic, and often emotional. That's why marketers love them, because consumers are not easy to figure out, and this keeps us on our toes. But these idiosyncrasies are also what should have business leaders sitting up and taking notice of customer data, for it is a dimension critical to their strategic planning. Hidden within consumer data is a wellspring of unmet needs and deep consumer insights that, when used properly across the organization, can carry a company to an advanced state of customer commitment. Data is at the heart of your ability to anticipate consumer needs, encourage desired behaviors, and, most importantly, recognize members in a way that is uniquely relevant.

This is the kind of information companies engaging in loyalty should be looking for: insights that reveal more than mere demographics—the inspirational triggers of a customer.

Data is at the heart of enterprise loyalty, and it marks a distinct evolution from a product- or channel-focused entity to a customer-centric one. The company's data strategy can do much more than feed product promotions and point balances. When done right, data can transform the company's go-to-market plan through optimized assortment, pricing, and store promotional strategies.

How to get there? First, think bigger. Recall the early days of the Internet, when a tiny percent of information was flowing through two-way communications and no one conceived that it would soon engulf us like a tsunami. In 1986, 14 percent of all landlines in the world were digital, but by 2007 that figure rose to 97 percent, and now we can't imagine life without digital communications.[1] Similarly, a company with customer data is sitting on a pipeline of information that never leaves the marketer's desk but would, if shared, change the way other parts of the enterprise see the customers. Enterprise loyalty uses the what, when, and where of customer behavior as a means to improving service and delivering an experience that is relevant.

Our coconuts to calling cards moment signaled the fact that we don't know everything about our customers, our services, or our operations. No one does. In fact, we may even be bringing an inherent bias into most of the analyses we undertake. The phrase "confirmation bias," in psychology and cognitive science, is defined as a tendency to "search for or interpret new information in a way that confirms one's preconceptions and to avoid information and interpretations that contradict prior beliefs."[2] Put another way: People tend to notice data that support their existing attitudes and beliefs, while ignoring or discrediting information that does not. The public's varying stances on global warming is a good example. Apply confirmation bias within an organization and we see that any perceived fault is not in the validity of the data set (customer data being a great example) but in the ability of other parts of the organization to accept data that is not in their "accepted metrics."

Yet if with even a distant vision of customer management, it stands to reason that customer data should add a new dimension to the company's operations. If that rich shopper information were in the building and being blocked behind a firewall, wouldn't it make sense to put it to work?

Let's explore how releasing this data across the organization leads to untapped opportunities in unexpected places, from the aisle to the in-box.

Setting Your Data Free

In essence, data collection is nothing more than the launch point for enterprise loyalty. Momentum is created only after that data is unleashed from the marketing department and set loose across the organization, so that it can be examined through a collective prism. Then, with the company's shared guidance, data can be put to work in nontraditional ways, meaning beyond marketing. Such efforts include real estate, pricing, staffing, and merchandising, as in our case of calling cards and coconuts. It's about putting the data to work in unexpected places.

And what better place to start than the casino? Caesars Entertainment, formerly known as Harrah's, bets on customer intimacy with data obtained from its more than forty-million-member

Total Rewards loyalty program and a firm understanding of what's required of its roughly seventy thousand employees.[3] This unbeatable combination has altered the face of the industry, and competitors are scrambling to catch up.

Like most reward programs, Total Rewards originated as a means of identifying and tracking the behavior of Caesars' gambling customers. But as the company observed how guests used the various Caesars brands, including Harrah's and Bally's, it uncovered substantial value opportunities in its nongambling visitors. Although these nongambling guests were not an obvious target, Caesars set out to capture information specifically about them, which meant rallying its employees in all departments and locations across the entire organization. As David Norton, the former chief marketing officer of Caesars (then Harrah's) explained:

> Early on in the process, we established that our customers are customers of the company, not of an individual property. This is important for a CRM [customer relationship marketing] strategy to work. Additionally, we placed an importance on business intelligence. The data we obtained showed us that a customer who visits multiple Harrah's properties spends more. So, in shared markets like Las Vegas where we have six properties, the revenue goal for all six properties is based on the performance of the market collectively. We encourage customers to stay within the Harrah's family if they are looking for different venues, as opposed to going to our competitors.[4]

Caesars does this by drawing complete customer profiles from the moment its guests enter the door and begin their experience. It uses this information to craft its products and services and then deliver them in a satisfying way. Caesars relies on its data to propel the strategy from an enterprisewide level, a critical input for designing the experience for its Total Rewards members and, in the process, all its customers. The data tells Caesars, for instance, that its Las Vegas residential customers expect a completely different experience from those who travel from across the country. Data have become critical in how Caesars creates strategic differentiation.

There are operational implications, no doubt—Caesars constantly modifies its data infrastructure to handle growth and assimilate new channels. And recently it added a technology that sends real-time offers to gamers while they play at the casino. But the starburst of knowledge it receives in return enables Caesars to modify its properties to match customer interests, whether they be for more table games, an increase in the number of a certain kind of machine, or a more diversified restaurant experience.

By embedding its customer insights into its strategic operations, Caesars placed its chips on data and won. Through its Total Rewards program, Caesars said in 2011, its properties were able to operate at a meaningful premium relative to its competitors—as high as 155 percent. It holds the number one or number two market share position in almost every major region where it operates and, in the first quarter of 2011, Caesars achieved a 55 percent customer satisfaction score, an all-time high. Further, Total Rewards helped enable its facilities in its key markets to generate considerable revenues from customers not originally playing at a select property while helping to increase repeat visitation and cross-market play, with $3 billion in 2010 companywide revenue from cross-property play.[5]

The same line of thinking can be applied to any industry, from travel to finance to retail.

Winning Hearts, from the Mailbox to the Aisle

Of course, data is not a homing pigeon, so simply collecting and releasing it across the organization does not mean it will reach your desired target. Each stakeholder has to engage with the customer to receive data, integrate it into standard operating practices, and then adapt the decision frameworks. There's the rub! We all have our preferred operating measures and data drivers, but the trick is not to search and replace. Customer intimacy means adding customer data to your existing management recipe, and spicing it up to invite customer loyalty.

Take the call center, where so much customer interaction takes place. Typical key performance indicators in the call center include: average call-handle time (AHT); call abandonment rate; call quality; and customer satisfaction. AHT is the big cost driver, but if you actually knew that your best customers were calling, and they had a high potential for up-sell to value-added services, and you knew what they were likely to buy, you could assess whether a longer call time was appropriate for these customers. Similarly, if your low-value customers are flooding the lines, you want to know that too. Chances are it's time to change your Web site to redirect the call flow to a lower-cost channel.

Winning the Customer with an Invisible Touch

But the call center isn't the only place where we interact with customers. With the growth of digital channels, social media, cell phone marketing, outsourced service providers, automated check-in, and countless other human and mechanized customer touch points, the data has got to flow seamlessly through the organization like blood pumping through the heart and to all limbs. Delivering a consistent customer experience across the multitude of these touch points takes work, and customer operations or marketing usually hold the key to synchronizing the experience across these encounters.

This exercise can be very complex for a bank or other financial institution whose many business units, product groups, and customer-marketing divisions all target the same customers. Barclaycard US faced this challenge when it examined the handling of its best customers. With forty cobranded card partners and roughly five million loyalty card members, Barclaycard realized that its proliferation of offers was actually causing unnecessary complexity and frustration for its loyal customers, because it was unknowingly sending competing offers for cobranded cards. So the company embarked on a connect-the-dots exercise to map the customer journey from the initial application through 250 touch points. Such efforts resulted in a companywide view of the end-to-end customer experience and how the financial institution's different departments could affect and enhance that encounter to support its own brand and its partner brands.[6]

As Michelle Bottomley, former chief marketing officer at Barclaycard US, put it:

> The challenge is to make sure these customer touch points have one voice, so it looks and feels like a part of the company—and we eliminated the ones that aren't necessary. That's part of taking the art and science approach of mapping out the customer experience. All of a sudden you can understand which ones are most important to creating customer satisfaction, which ones really drive whether customers are happy with you or not, and which ones are most important for us to address first.[7]

These lessons helped Barclaycard US eliminate the areas that caused customer frustration and reduce unnecessary cost while increasing customer margin by targeting the right products to the most receptive customers. Through the practice of enterprise loyalty, Barclaycard's journey through the customer experience now informs every decision of the business.

Getting to Know You . . .

But data absorption looks very different in the market research department. Frankly, I've always been amazed by the fact that customer attitudinal research and analytics are rarely dance partners, when the partnership of behaviors and attitudes makes so much sense. Imagine the power of knowing on a consistent basis where your customers go, what they do, and—most important—how they feel about it.

In this way, data has the power to differentiate the customer experience, from the way we are treated by the call center associate to the dressing room experience. But while some of our functions can be tailored to the customer, there are others, such as R&D, assortment, and pricing, which are more challenging to execute at the individual level, at least in major retail.

To understand how to make enterprise loyalty work tactically, it helps to examine the ways in which it can be applied to the many divisions and disciplines of an organization's operations. Let's walk through them.

Real Estate: Building Competitive Advantages One Brick (and Mortar) at a Time

Many retailers use their online or catalog customer data to determine new store locations. They simply run algorithms to identify clusters of customers by region, cross-reference those figures with shopping patterns (average transaction, frequency, and price sensitivity), and then use the findings to determine future brick-and-mortar locations.

Well, what about the locational data of neighboring businesses? Data-sharing opportunities have helped brick-and-mortar chains gang together when new competitors enter their markets. Consider the case of RONA Inc., Canada's biggest home improvement chain in 2011 with about 20 percent of market share and plans to grow to 25 percent.[8] RONA operated more than 950 stores of various formats, generating sales north of $6 billion. Still, the company—an AIR MILES coalition partner—does not take its leadership position for granted and is ever watchful about who is moving into the neighborhood.

So when Home Depot planned an expansion into RONA's trade areas in and around Quebec back in 2005, the retailer turned on the loyalty data tap. RONA already knew through its financial analysis and ongoing market research that whenever a Home Depot opened locations in a RONA market, nearby stores suffered double-digit sales declines within weeks. But RONA had one advantage over Home Depot, and that was the customer data it acquired through its participation in a loyalty program. Since that program happened to be within the AIR MILES coalition, the information was augmented by a network of partners that together could provide a combined incentive to encourage customers to continue to shop at RONA. Either way, the data in its customer database was critical to structuring an early defense plan to counteract exactly where Home Depot was opening its new stores.

RONA had already identified the affected stores by examining where its own shoppers lived in proximity to the Home Depot stores. Next it picked its partners for a data alliance, something any business could do to gain alignment with noncompetitive categories in its markets. Were those RONA shoppers more likely to visit the gas station just up the street? What about the supermarket two miles away? Once it was able to identify these shared merchants, RONA invited them to join a program wherein they would offer special rewards to customers for coming in to RONA for two weeks before and four weeks after the Home Depot opening. These participating members also distributed coupons.

The power of partners, and shared data, worked. Instead of the forecasted 10 percent to 15 percent decline in sales, RONA stores experienced no sales decline at all. In fact, the average transaction size of those consumers who used the offer increased by an average of 8 percent in the affected period. And total sales among loyalty program participants rose by 5 percent.

Clearly it pays to have good neighbors, good data, and a willingness to share it with your regular business partners. Doing so opens a window into your shoppers' activities once they leave your store or location.

Formatting: Size, and Shape, Matter

As much as customer data helps improve store location decisions, it is equally necessary in optimizing store formats. Remember the Shell case study? The use of customer data enabled the fuel chain to identify which stores it could close with the least bit of sales loss and disruption and which to transform or relocate into larger, more updated formats. The result of its data-driven strategy was higher sales at both existing and new locations.

This level of trade-area analysis, based on customer data, gives companies the means to profile customers on the basis of an individual store, branch, or office and then identify the gaps in activity. Merchants can then use this customer picture to identify opportunities for differentiation, innovation, and services by location. Sure, the company could buy demographic data from a local research provider and overlay it on a store map, but it is missing an essential ingredient: the customer's actual purchasing information. Target Corp., for example, in 2012 plans to open a small-format concept it calls CityTarget. These stores will operate in urban areas, including downtown Chicago, and complement the traditional Target stores as well as the suburban SuperTargets that added full grocery selections to their usual array. The plan is to apply the CityTarget nameplate to other urban, small-format locations, such as its stores in New York and Seattle.[9]

Target is not the only retailer employing this strategy. Walmart, Tesco, and Sainsbury all tailor their store formatting based on customer behavior, as does the Indian retailer Shoppers Stop.

Shoppers Stop uses its customer insights to inform location-by-location merchandising and store expansion planning. "We're at thirty-four stores, and we plan to almost double that number to sixty in the next three years," Vinay Bhatia, vice president of marketing and loyalty, told COLLOQUY in 2011. The chain used data analysis to locate and shape a store in Amritsar, in the north of India, after such insights revealed Amritsar residents were shopping at a Shoppers Stop in Delhi. "We knew exactly what people in Amritsar were buying. When we went into the new location, there was no trial and error in terms of appealing to local tastes," Bhatia said.

Similar analysis helped Shoppers Stop predict the impact of new store openings in existing markets. Using a model to anticipate the level of cannibalization, it knew the effect a new store would have on nearby locations and also learned it could reduce staffing and the density of merchandise from location to location.

The new store, meanwhile, also benefited. "We opened a store in an area of Mumbai called Vashi, and there were two contiguous stores nearby," Bhatia said. "We looked at what the Vashi customers were buying at the other stores, and we saw that they were buying a higher mix of accessories—footwear and other nonapparel. Due to that insight, we created a much larger beauty and cosmetics hall in the Vashi store, and that store is doing very well for us."[10]

By using data to recognize the behavioral patterns of shoppers, organizations can figure out not only which store format best suits a location, but also the type of merchandise that would be in demand, and the floor layout that would be conducive to the lifestyle requirements of shoppers in that immediate vicinity.

Selection: My Closet Is Full, but There's Nothing to Wear

In our own quest for enterprisewide customer-data integration, LoyaltyOne's associates and executives have toured many of the data hubs across the company. The call centers benefited from adapting service on the basis of customer value; market research became smarter through deeper insights; the marketing department was better able to fight the competition; and real estate developed store formats based on customer behaviors. But what about the traditionalists in merchandising? They've been in the business for years, and there is nothing that customer data can tell them that they don't already know. Or maybe there is. Let's travel now to South Africa, home to the Woolworths hypermarket chain, which combines supermarket with a department store format.

Woolworths uses rewards program data to analyze and identify key customer segments and determine which products are most important to each. In one effort to better serve its patrons while also finessing its merchandise mix and understanding the in-store experience, the merchant isolated each segment's core purchases from its discretionary purchases and then adjusted its product assortment based on its findings.

Woolworths, which highlighted its findings at the National Retail Federation's annual convention in New York in 2008, increased its sales by 6 percent, as a result of these insights, but not by adding products to its stores. Instead, it removed 15 percent of the merchandise that its research showed was not relevant to its most profitable customer segments. It therefore spent more time promoting and merchandising an optimized product mix.[11]

The takeaway is that delivering what the consumer wants takes a combination of data analysis and on-the-floor intelligence. The day is coming when you will be at a disadvantage if you don't have access to customer metrics. Let's compare the experience of Woolworths with Walmart. In 2010 Walmart pulled hundreds of slower-moving items from its shelves, in order to enhance its selection of merchandise. But Walmart's "SKU rationalization" to reduce the number of items on its shelves actually eliminated products that were important to its best shoppers, resulting in lost sales. Walmart ended up restocking three hundred to four hundred of those items, but if it had had the relevant data available through a loyalty program, it might have avoided the issue all together.[12]

Pricing and Promotions: Turning Habits into Passion

The next stop is pricing, an area of the retail business that requires high analytical skills and experience in building complex price-sensitivity models. Pricing is critical to influencing consumer consideration and purchasing, so it is a prime example of a merchandising practice that is significantly upgraded with customer data.

Few items in the store aisle get as much price scrutiny as cereal. Retailers know this. So when LoyaltyOne analysts were asked to identify how the price of cereal affected the shopping patterns of their best customers, we knew where to look in the customer data. The goal was to develop a pricing strategy that maximized both category and shopper profitability. Our approach was simple: We scored the cereal in two categories, one based on the brand's importance to priority shoppers and the other on the shoppers' price sensitivities. And we found (drum roll, please) that many of the cereals were not priced to move. Case in point: We saw that many of the brands shoppers were very price sensitive to were expensive relative to the competition. Meantime, the retailer charged much less for cereal brands that shoppers would willingly pay more for.

We recommended a variation on Willy Wonka's phrase "Strike that. Reverse it." First we suggested that the retailer change its pricing strategy on those more expensive cereals and switch them to everyday low pricing, in order to improve cost perceptions and increase customer loyalty. Next we suggested it raise the price of those cereals shoppers were willing to spend more on and then promote them at a discount only when attempting to drive traffic in key periods. With our plan the retailer was able to boost category margins through more effective pricing.[13]

There are a variety of promotional tools merchants can use to influence customer behavior and lift sales. Flier distribution is considered old school in the digital age, but it is still a cost-effective way to market locally, mainly because they carry weekly product promotions that pull customers into stores. That said, there is an opportunity to fortify this traditional channel with customer data, by shaping both its content and the neighborhood distribution. Customer information can help to determine which product or service offer will cause consumers to make stock-up shopping trips, compared with those that will trigger a replenishment trip for staples such as milk and eggs, pens and paper, or shampoo and conditioner. Purchasing behavior helps distinguish big planned trips from those quick hits on the way home from the office. It helps determine why shoppers will traverse an entire store to buy two seemingly disparate items, like coconuts and calling cards, but will not purchase products that are side by side. While shopper behaviors may sometimes seem to defy logic, customer data combined with the right analytical tools can reveal the patterns behind customer choice; if you tease the insights enough, you can get them to tell you most anything you need.

New Products and Services: When R&D Means Rich with Data

I know some marketers think that R&D means rip-off and duplicate, but to me it should mean rich with data. I am always on the lookout for great examples of companies leveraging their deep data sets to drive innovation in product development, and you can bet your best customers that organizations like Kroger, Walmart, Best Buy, and just about any major online retailer have got it covered.

Among such organizations, and one that I have personally visited, is Recyclebank. The New York–based company rewards points to people who recycle and reduce their energy use. It has aligned itself with hundreds of municipalities that deploy collection bins retrofitted with tracking devices. The weight of the recycled materials is recorded at pickup and credited to the recycler's account. Members, in turn, can redeem these accumulated points with more than twenty-six hundred merchant partners, including CVS, Friskies, Kashi, and Bed, Bath & Beyond.

By combining loyalty data with a cause, Recyclebank has created a market where one did not previously exist. Between 2005—the year it was founded—and 2010 more than two million members throughout the United States and the UK joined Recyclebank's loyalty program and earned reward points for recycling plastics, mailing in their old electronics, and choosing a wind-based electricity supplier. These members and communities were responsible for saving more than ten million trees and 672 million gallons of oil in that time. Along the way, municipalities participating in the Recyclebank program have saved millions of dollars in landfill diversion fees.[14]

Do You Hear What I Hear? The Customer's Voice

At this point it should be evident that customer data, when used well, adds value and deepens customer commitment, and that it can create more effective operations wherever it lands within the organization. But data collection is only a first step. The business also needs to engage consumers. Yes, that's right: It's important to talk to your customers. It's also important to hear them respond, to provide feedback, ideas, and thoughts—and not only on those occasions when they are disappointed with the product or service. Such interactions, particularly positive ones, take emotional engagement.

A few important considerations are necessary to achieving this level of customer commitment, or enterprise loyalty:

- **Not all customers are created equal.** The needs of high-profit, high-potential customers should be recognized. It sounds glaringly obvious, but in most organizations the marketing department is the only group that has rethought business practices. Call centers, operations, market research, real estate, merchandising, and product development—take heed!

- **Share the load with your partners.** There are ways to share customer insights and information that do not put you in harm's way with privacy advocates. The first step is to be clear and straightforward with your members about how the data is to be used, and why (and not in itty-bitty copy, please). In fact, when done right you can add value and relevance to customers and build strategic partnerships with companies in noncompeting categories in your backyard.

- **Conversations are a two-way street.** It's time to boost customer engagement and interactions. This is the natural next step: progressing from merely identifying and tracking customers to engaging them in dialogue. These interactions are triggered when the company gathers and then responds to shared customer preferences and other information in a social or community environment. Companies can achieve a trialogue that amplifies the value and reach of the customers' voices by leveraging their ability to share opinions on a massive scale within social media networks.

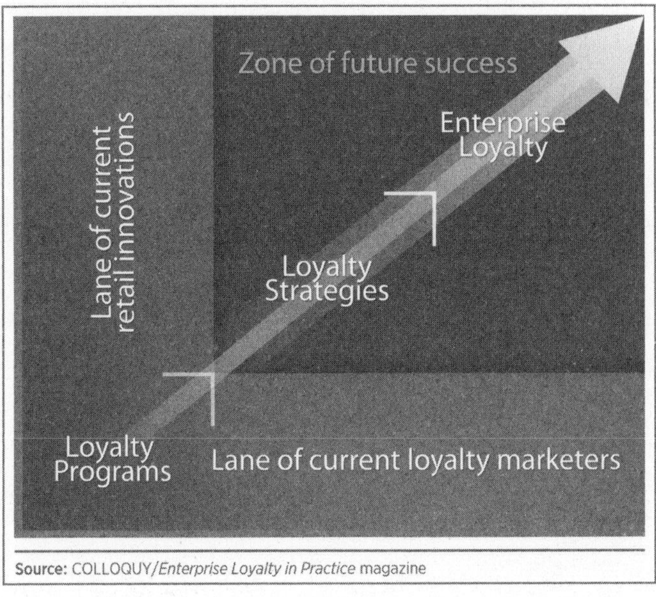

Source: COLLOQUY/*Enterprise Loyalty in Practice* magazine

So it comes down to sharing communications beyond the boundaries of the company, and this includes conversations with suppliers and other partners whose information could help all parties benefit the customer. Merchants and their partners not only hear their customers' ideas but also learn each other's thoughts on potential new services, products, or plans. Customers can play a role in determining store closures or renovations, merchandise choices, store formats, and even office hours.

One company that has made a real technological splash with its partners is Coca-Cola, with its Freestyle soda fountain machines. The fountains, which have been installed in participating fast-food and restaurant chains, serve 125 different soft drinks, flavored waters, sports drinks, and lemonades, and then send the usage data, including which flavors are most popular at different times of day, to Coca-Cola headquarters. By the fall of 2011 fifteen hundred machines were supplying information from chains including Wendy's, Burger King, and Firehouse Subs, the last of which credited the fountains for a double-digit increase in sales. The data is mixed and matched by both Coke and its restaurant customers to provide a clear picture of consumer trends, such as the popularity of Caffeine-Free Diet Coke after 3:00 P.M. Consumers, meanwhile, latched on to the technology: The presence of a Freestyle fountain would likely cause 20 percent to switch restaurants or convenience stores.[15]

This vignette illustrates how sharing your innovations as well as your data can enhance both the customer experience and the bottom line. In doing so companies like Coca-Cola are achieving loyalty with a big L.

And you do need that big L for enterprise loyalty to work. If traditional database marketing results in direct-to-consumer communications and changed behavior, then enterprise loyalty extends the application of data to those thought processes that have customarily been operationally focused. Simply put, enterprise loyalty brings the application of data to areas of the company that have rarely or never before used such information to guide their decisions.

Of course, while data helps facilitate these discussions, they will not ring true without buy in from your flesh-and-blood people. Employees are an indispensable source for making enterprise loyalty happen. If your staff is not engaged in your company, then they probably aren't going to be loyal to it. And if they don't feel that loyalty it is unlikely they'll be able to capture the interest, and hearts, of your customers.

CHAPTER 8

Employee Loyalty: How Do I Build a Customer-Centric Culture?

It's a long-held view that you can't love your customers if you don't love your employees, and a corollary to that is that you can't win customer loyalty if you haven't earned employee loyalty. Early on in my career, when I was totally focused on the value of marketing science, I drank a little too heavily from the fountain of direct-to-consumer marketing and believed that the bulk of the company's efforts should be put into targeting the right customers with a strategy effective enough to change their behaviors. I had understood the value of frontline execution, having worked as a sales and merchandising intern one summer in packaged goods, but I started to think that strong planning and program management could control frontline work sufficiently to make it inconsequential.

For a period I forgot my grassroots experiences and missed the blindingly obvious point: You can't change customer behavior if you are not affecting employee behavior. More important, genuinely engaged employees deliver something that strategy and effective execution never will, and that's heart. The sensitivity and spontaneity of human interaction picks up where science fails us. That is why they call it "relationship" management. So, many years back, when AIR MILES had grown so large that decision making and delivery were largely decentralized, I became a reformed scientist and a marketer with a newfound respect for frontline delivery in general and in my team, which delivers our services, in particular.

Over the years, a few other teams have earned my respect as well. Among them are those at Zappos.com, a company renowned for its quirky, free-spirited culture, and one that estimates its repeat customers represent about 70 percent of its daily business.

Zappos.com counts roughly three thousand reasons for this high figure, five hundred of whom are on the front lines in its call center every day.

The correlation between happy customers and happy workers is pretty fundamental to Zappos.com's leadership, which recognizes that its high shopper loyalty is a natural by-product of its healthy work culture. To Rob Siefker, director of the customer loyalty team, the dedication of Zappos.com's staff is won through great experiences that engender a bond with the brand.

"We want them to feel emotionally engaged, not just because we want them to be efficient and productive, but because we want them to feel that they're contributing something to the business; that they're growing individually," Siefker told us in a 2011 phone interview. "We want them to be passionate about what they do."

Zappos.com has gained national attention for the thoughtful perks it provides, including free lunches and the presence of a full-time life coach. When CEO Tony Hsieh wrote his book, *Delivering Happiness,* he had more than customers in mind.

Tangible employee benefits are the price, but trust is something you can't buy. The amount of trust Zappos.com bestows upon its employees is remarkable, especially the extent to which the company allows employees to make in-the-moment judgments that define customers' experiences. By doing so the company is essentially putting its operational and financial controls in the hands of its front line. Workers do not need permission to resolve a customer's issue or to extend a sign of appreciation, regardless of whether the decision involves free shoes, company credit, or even a bouquet of flowers. Zappos.com does not even have a system of procedures in place for employees to seek such permission. Usually workers just ask for a second opinion, and they are typically advised to trust themselves.

The tools for resolving any such issues are equally intangible. For one thing, Zappos.com does not restrict average call-handling time. Calls can take twenty minutes or (in at least one case) eight hours, which can have significant cost implications. As it turns out, the average call hovers at five minutes. But when calls do last longer, the time is justified, because it is used to establish a real connection with customers and to learn about the caller's needs—for her travels, a recent birthday, or a coming adventure.

Reading between the lines it seems as though, in the early days of the company, a choice was made between investment in data collection and people, and, as a result, Zappos.com's data-collection abilities were limited. The company instead relied on its supply chain, Web capabilities, and—significantly—the judgment of all its workers. That is changing now, as Zappos.com is actively investing in customer-data management, but Siefker does not doubt the company's decision to invest in its employees and their phone time first. "If they're not the right people, it doesn't matter what we give them," he said. "It starts with creating the right home, the right culture, the right environment here. Then everything else we want to accomplish is much easier."

Online companies such as Zappos.com have mastered the task of delivering a high-touch experience in a high-tech environment. It is a dazzling example of putting a face on a brand.

Unfortunately, to many companies both online and offline, the expression of their brand exists in a logo, a Web site design, or a distinctive store layout but not in a human "face." Yet it is the human presence that remains most clearly fixed in the customer's mind—a cashier, a sales-floor associate, or even a voice on the phone. To be remembered, a brand has to be experienced. Better than any roadside billboard, it is that personal interaction that drives memory and brand association. The customer's last recollection of that interaction recalibrates his or her perception of a company's value. So every time employees interact with customers, the company's value is being assessed or reassessed.

The oversimplified resolution to such complex encounters is to provide consistency in service. The unavoidable wrinkle is the highly unpredictable nature of human behavior. Organizations are recognizing the shift in customer attitudes about service. According to a 2011 survey by Forrester Research, 90 percent of executives think customer experience is very important or critical for their companies, while 80 percent are trying to use it as an area of differentiation.[1] Yet only half of the 118 customer-experience professionals surveyed said they had a companywide program to improve the customer experience across channels, and only 30 percent had dedicated a budget to fund such efforts.

This speaks to a rather vexing issue in executive decision making: The management of human interactions, be they with employees or customers, is an inexact science. Developing *consistent* experiences—not necessarily great experiences—is like removing production errors from your manufacturing process. It can be planned, measured, and quantified. But delivering a memorable customer experience, or giving employees the tools and latitude to humanize the brand, is foreign territory for many company executives. Having spent years comparing customer survey results to loyalty measures within our company and for our partners, I have come to this conclusion: Service consistency is required but banal. Service inconsistency, better defined as "unprompted" experiences, is what drives brand brilliance. This is the territory Zappos.com claimed as a differentiator, and we all should be shooting for some measure of unscripted experiences in everything we do.

Any meaningful efforts first require personal, or personnel, appreciation. Employee satisfaction is tantamount to achieving your company goals. If your workers are not happy they simply will not carry out your game plan, leaving you ten yards short of the goal to customer engagement.

The methods an organization uses to position and enable its frontline staff are what separate the successful from the truly brilliant. Put customer information at employees' fingertips and they will be provided with the tools to create better customer experiences. The more relevant the information, the better equipped they will be to make on-the-spot decisions that will translate into meaningful customer encounters. These positive experiences boost employee morale, inspiring your workers to become company ambassadors and the torchbearers of enterprise loyalty.

Where does this lead? That is up to you. Technological innovations are inspiring a spectrum of customer service enhancements, from immediate knowledge of a guest's last travel destination to interactive mirrors in retailer dressing rooms.

Combine these advancements with the boundless creativity of engaged employees and the future is ours to determine.

Happy Spouse, Happy House: The Relationship Between Employees and Profitability

No doubt about it, employees drive customer return on investment; engaged employees will create engaged, and therefore loyal, customers. I've already shared the equation for lifetime customer value (projected annual sales multiplied by the number of years the customer is expected to shop with the company). But in a recent article in *Harvard Business Review*, that value was put into dollars: A loyal pizza eater's lifetime revenue can be $8,000, while a Cadillac owner's is closer to $332,000.

These figures are used to support a model called the "service-profit chain" described in the article by James Heskett, Harvard professor emeritus, Gary Loveman, now CEO of Caesars Entertainment, and several others.[2]

The service-profit chain establishes the relationships between profitability, customer loyalty, and employee satisfaction (the latter of which results in loyalty and productivity). The following image illustrates the point: Profit and growth are fueled by customer loyalty. Loyalty results from customer satisfaction. This satisfaction is influenced by the value of your product or service, which in turn is created by happy, loyal, and productive employees. Last, employee satisfaction results from support services and policies that enable them to deliver results that foster pride.

This lesson brings to my mind the old adage "happy spouse,

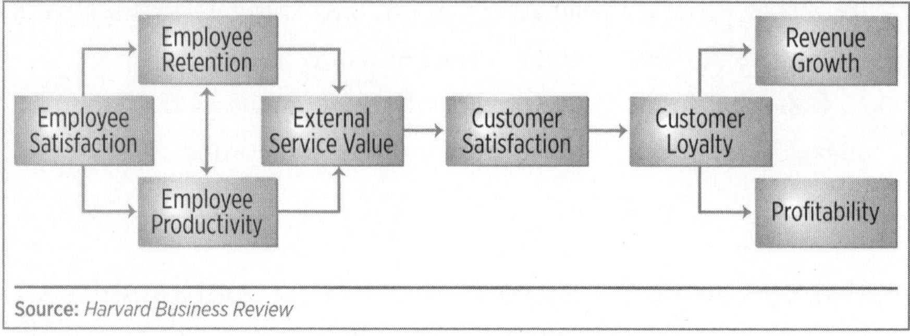

Source: *Harvard Business Review*

happy house." If you can create appropriate associate engagement, then your workers will gladly play a vital role in creating higher sales and profits from your customers. Sounds like loyalty, doesn't it?

Bringing Corner-Store Service to the Mega Mall

The challenge, increasingly, is maintaining the emotional loyalty of thousands of consumers who may pass relatively unknown though our doors. Remember the days, a few generations ago, when the experience between customer and business was completely personal? Before industries began to merge and form major national and international corporations most merchants understood the needs of their customers, as well as the events of their immediate families, on a firsthand basis.

Today the corner store, just like the family doctors of our childhoods, exists primarily in television reruns. And just as the store clerk knew your hat size and cigarette preference, your doctor tended to all of your needs, both physical and emotional. But today we operate in a world of specialists, and we don't have the same emotional ties.

Our jobs are made more difficult by the complexity of our systems and the scale of our delivery. We manage hundreds of processes, thousands of employees, and millions of customers. Acting with consistency requires buttoned-down processes and trained employees. But acting "inconsistently," or enabling seemingly random acts of spontaneity such as remembering a customer's graduation date or sending her a wardrobe idea—that takes employee passion, and it leads to heightened intimacy and memorable interactions.

Consider the case of Macy's Inc., a chain of more than eight hundred locations, and its stores in Chicago. Back in 2009 the department store chain took a walk in its customers' shoes, and I mean that literally. In a conference with analysts at Goldman Sachs, Macy's CEO Terry Lundgren explained how he learned that the number one request at the Macy's Chicago stores was for size eleven women's shoes. There just were not enough of them.

This demand was surprising. Size eleven is just not a common shoe size for women. As Lundgren put it himself, *he* wears a size eleven shoe.[3]

In fact, the demand might not have become evident if it were not for the My Macy's merchandising program, a localization effort that breaks the chain's vast network of stores into geographic segments that are each overseen by buyers and planners who are in the aisles. In Chicago, when these buyers and planners heard about the frequent requests for size eleven shoes, they had the information and flexibility to react to this product opportunity. They created a complete display of size eleven shoes, with twenty different styles in all. It was the first time Macy's had organized a display by size, but that's what customers wanted, and it worked. The store was selling six and seven pairs at a time, Lundgren said.

Through top-to-bottom customer alignment Macy's found that even a small percentage of shoppers represented a significant market. Its response demonstrated that it understood their needs and could meet them. According to Donald Sull, a professor of strategic and international management at the London Business School, companies walk past lucrative opportunities all the time, usually because they don't notice data or pay attention to subtle clues in their experience. Several of his "10 Clues to Opportunity" involve customer signals that we're not equipped to recognize. The clues for Macy's would be: "Customers shouldn't want this product (but they do)" and "Customers have discovered a product (but not the one we offer)."[4]

How do you deliver this kind of experience when you have so many employees serving the same customer without really knowing who she is and her history with you? It is a challenge more easily overcome in the airline and hospitality business, where a guest's name will pop up in the computer on check-in. But in other major industries, most notably retail, there can be real anonymity in the aisles. According to a 2010 Grocery Manufacturers Association study of consumer packaged goods (CPG), "Shopper marketing—efforts to observe and influence shoppers at the time of purchase—is one of the hottest and fastest-growing activities in advertising and promotions."[5] But because CPG makers are not in direct control of the customer experience in the aisles, that relationship belongs to the retailer, which can take advantage of opportunities to personalize the store visit.

Among those is Safeway, which in 2011 rolled out an elite program for shoppers who spent more than $125 a week. When these high-value, targeted customers scan their loyalty card at the cash register, the manager is notified by text and can personally approach the customer with a package of value-added offers that say "thanks for your continued patronage." In addition, elite members get discounts on fuel, flowers, and deli sandwiches, cash back, refunds without receipts, and—in a truly distinguishing move—the store manager's cell phone number.[6]

Company Anonymity Quiz: Who Are You?

There are ways to put faces on the crowd without crossing the creepy line. The trick is to remember that your reason for identifying customers is to deliver a heightened experience. To that end, all strategies should be test run to gauge how they connect with and support frontline performance.

This is especially the case when you run "overt" and "covert" strategies that are used first to market a product and second to reinforce your underlying message through motivational communications. Frontline employees need to be schooled in the subtlety of delivering these communications and offers.

The instruments in the strategic toolbox I find most effective for customer communications are targeted offers that someone would receive based on his or her activity with the company. These can be delivered through any channel, from text message to e-mail to direct mail. For starters, employees should be informed of offers before they hit the street, but even better is asking employees to support the offer with additional information, and even authorizing them to upgrade the offer based on needs. That sounds great in a project plan, I know, but can it be executed?

In business-to-business marketing, for example, execution is less of a challenge, because each salesperson has a sense of the allotted wiggle room in negotiating sales promotions on the fly. In consumer marketing we are more heavily reliant on overt tools such as conventional mass communications, which include the Web, print media, and direct marketing. For consumer, retail, or financial services promotions, employees are expected to fulfill the offer as communicated, but there is little room for variability unless the customer asks for an upgrade, which usually involves a higher authority, like a branch manager.

This is often the reason why companies get involved in loyalty programs. Most loyalty program structures are built for flexible brand experiences through tiered loyalty. They send an explicit communication that says "Increase your business with us and we'll give you more value."

Tiered loyalty structures provide recognition benefits to your best customers based on their spending and service thresholds, which are helpful guides to your workers. These programs are not new—many organizations, from airlines to hotels to department stores, use tiered plans to provide a personalized experience to their most loyal customers. But few organizations use tiered plans as a tool for employees to enhance the customer experience.

Neiman Marcus's InCircle rewards program, for instance, has six tiers, all the way up to Chairman's Circle. Here luxury shoppers who spend at least $600,000 a year receive complimentary in-store alterations, dining, parking, fur storage, and delivery from Neiman Marcus or Bergdorf Goodman. All perks are hand-delivered by an associate who would know that guest on a first-name basis. At a lower earning level, all members from Circle Three up have InCircle Access, an exclusive benefit that provides one-of-a-kind VIP travel offers. Want front-row seats at a Knicks game? Maybe dinner at Mugaritz in Spain, or Alinea in Chicago? Or perhaps one of the limited-edition fur vests that match your Burberry raincoat? Neiman's employees will find it and win your undying gratitude in the process.

But a company does not have to be in the luxury space to use tiers as instruments of exceptional employee service. Best Buy's two-tiered program offers its own top-shelf, or Premier Silver, level for shoppers who spend just $2,500 a year, which equates to a flat-screen TV, a digital video camera, and maybe a few handset upgrades. Among Premier Silver perks: invitations to see movies before they're released; exclusive access to special events; a complimentary Geek Squad home theater consultation; and access to the around-the-clock Premier Silver help line. These benefits promise an elevated level of recognition, but they also provide Best Buy associates opportunities to connect and build relationships with their customers.

And for an incredibly high-touch tier approach, there's Caesars Entertainment. The casino and resort operator offers levels all the way up to Seven Star, which is so exclusive that members must be invited to join by their casino host. Caesars could not make this customer commitment without flawless execution. Gamblers at this level walk on water and are treated with the utmost care by all casino workers. No lines, no wait times, no worries. These members get one free trip to Caesars every year, including airfare, hotel, and all the extras.

Next Question: Do You Know Where Bureaucracy Lives?

Coming back down to earth and the complexities of employee management, it's worth noting that tiered loyalty programs do not work on autopilot. You've made overt commitments to your customers, and failure is not an option. To be successful these programs need you to stand up and be counted. The best way to infuse your people with the customer-committed attitude that is enterprise loyalty is to adopt it yourself.

Doing so requires steadfast attention to the layer of management that exists between you and your frontline employees. This is where process issues, legal requirements, financial controls, technology snags, and a host of other corporate disjointedness originates. In my experience, the process layer is where bureaucracy lives. My apologies for being trite, but you're either part of the problem or part of the solution. As leaders, it's for us to decide.

This means our leadership must communicate not only customer intimacy goals but also customer outcomes and their direct link to success. I'm not talking mealymouthed e-mails or an announcement in the break room. Rather, this level of buy-in takes the structured, ongoing reinforcement of a companywide customer embrace. Top management may write its own version of the customer experience story, but involving employees in a way that motivates them takes *teaching*, not training. And your teaching should be shared with all employees who have a role in the employee experience, which I bet is most if not all of them.

Lastly, try teaching by example. Make heroes of those who apply sound judgment and think with their hearts, and inspire your workers to do the same. Remember the three Rs for achieving loyalty among your customers: rewards, recognition, and relevance. These three factors are equally necessary in achieving dedication from your employees.

Consider again the case of Caesars. In shared markets like Las Vegas, where it operates multiple properties, Caesars bases its revenue goals on the performance of the collective market, not just of one location. So Caesars compensates its employees accordingly, with incentives that ensure that marketwide sales and guest satisfaction are recognized and rewarded.

The third R, relevance, will ensure your ability to relate to both your employee and customer experiences. One of our AIR MILES sponsors, UPS, would require that all its managers, and any of our employees working on its business, spend at least one day in uniform riding with a UPS driver. The job entails delivering packages, talking to customers, and loading vans. This quality of relevance also comes to life through the training programs at USAA, a company that provides financial services and insurance to military families. According to a story in *BusinessWeek*:

> New reps attend sessions where they dine on MREs, or "meals ready to eat," which troops consume in the field. They try on Kevlar vests and flak helmets. And each rep is handed a bona fide deployment letter—with the names changed, of course—to get them [*sic*] thinking about the financial decisions customers face at such an emotional time. Colleen Williams, a Phoenix-based service rep who joined the company in 2008, says the training clued her in to family issues that help her when answering calls. "I speak to women who haven't talked to their husbands in six weeks," she says. "It never really registered to me, the real disconnect" deployed soldiers have from their families.[7]

Making Heroes of Your Workers: How to Empower Employees

This kind of effective training is actually storytelling, and if you don't believe me, try to remember the contents of the last three PowerPoint presentations you attended. Even when formal training programs are designed to solidly ensure company performance, they typically lack the flexibility to accept employee input or troubleshooting.

One of my work associates had such an experience recently when visiting an area location of a national restaurant chain one weekend for breakfast with three friends. They each ordered a breakfast that came with blueberry crêpes, eggs, bacon, and fruit. It was a great deal, except that three of them did not eat pork, and one was a vegetarian. Thinking it was an easy-to-fix problem, they asked the server if they could just exchange the bacon for anything else. He said they could—with ham or sausage.

Obviously these options did not appeal to them, so they suggested some extra fruit instead—anything else would do. But the server turned them down, explaining that their choices were bacon, sausage, ham, or nothing. My associate asked to speak with a manager, who politely explained that the corporate office had stopped offering nonmeat substitutions, despite push-back from managers. He clearly did not think it was a good practice.

Here's the kicker: Before they departed the manager suggested that the four of them call the head office themselves, "because they really care about what the customer has to say."

In the end, caring about the customer is only half of the equation.

Enterprise loyalty is about liberating your employees to be spontaneous customer advocates. Just like you need to set data free across the organization, it's time to free your associates to use their teaching, talent, and common sense to move the company forward.

It is a concept well in practice at AIR MILES. Like Zappos.com, we have unshackled our associates from the standard measures of call time, preferring that they focus instead on creating an engaging experience with our Collectors, or program members. Through an approach we call the "customer experience blueprint," we encourage associates to approach all of their Collector encounters as an opportunity to demonstrate value, even when the Collector isn't sure what he or she is looking for.

By exploring Collector needs our associates can at the same time prevent potential disappointments, such as the unavailability of a desired flight.

In practice, the program is built on three pillars:

- **Engage and discover:** We acknowledge the Collector and personalize the call by asking questions relevant to understanding his or her goal, and to gauging possible flexibility. If we learn that the Collector is traveling for a very important business meeting, for instance, we might suggest that an earlier flight would give him a few hours to prepare. Or we may probe to identify other unexpressed requests and use the information to add value later in the interaction.
- **Solve the initial need with value:** We address the request or issue with options that would resolve it, underscoring the benefit of each alternative. Flexible travel dates? Traveling with a wheelchair? The AIR MILES employee thinks on his feet about solutions that provide value and are useful and relevant to the member's situation. No point in suggesting a family trip on a week that's cheaper if school's not out.
- **Relate value:** The associate explains the value of each of the options and provides tips to further ease the next

> interaction with AIR MILES. "Did you know that booking two weeks earlier would have guaranteed availability?" We then end the call by making sure there's nothing else on the Collector's mind. We never put the Collector on hold. Instead, we put him on "open hold," staying on the line and chatting through the booking, while also asking questions to deepen the experience. "Oh, this is an annual event? Good to know."

The customer feedback has been compelling. Through customer research ten years ago we learned that the worst thing we could do was transfer a call, because it made customers feel disconnected. Our call center specialists reconnect them and have been rewarded with satisfaction rates that rank in the top 5 percent of 350 leading North American call centers, based on a survey by Service Quality Measurement.[8] And in our own annual in-house employee satisfaction surveys, 84 percent of our call center associates said they were either satisfied or very satisfied, one of the highest ratings in the company.

The Piper Plays the Tune. Pay the Piper.

Good value to customers also translates into good value for employees, so don't expect superior employee engagement for inferior compensation. At the upscale Fairmont Hotels & Resorts, the happy house is underscored by its mission of "turning moments into memories for our guests." Fairmont does this by providing what it describes as "authentically local" experiences through the warm and engaging service of its colleagues. To pull this off, Fairmont puts trust in the hands of its frontline employees.

Fairmont President's Club is a means to collect pertinent information about guest preferences, which is then provided to employees so they can tailor experiences that are relevant and rewarding. In turn, Fairmont's Service Plus Memory Maker recognition program lets guests and others nominate employees for exceptional thoughtfulness and service. The winners were recognized ceremoniously and could redeem their choice of award from thousands of merchants globally.[9] Fairmont's best customers, meanwhile, were invited to engage in a recognition program and celebrate great service.

Likewise, at USAA, call center agents received 2009 bonuses that represented almost 19 percent of their pay, up from 13.5 percent the previous year. But time is also money, so USAA offers workers a five-dollar-an-hour concierge service, so employees can outsource their personal errands during the workday.

You Mean Coffee and Doughnuts Aren't Enough?

The takeaway is that if you want employee engagement, loyalty, and reduced turnover, you will need to build compensation programs that recognize their specific skills in accomplishing your expectations.

Market leaders such as Caesars, Fairmont, USAA, and others use measurement and incentive structures that reinforce the desired frontline behaviors for promoting and supporting each company's specific customer engagement and intimacy strategy.

At the same time, these recognition and measurement programs should extend all the way up and through the organization. If frontline employees are tethered by the same process layer that outlawed vegetarian options on the breakfast plate, then we need incentives to break these middle-management barriers.

This kind of systemic compensation structure could also become a key ingredient in the change-management process.

If You Want Employees to Drive Loyalty, Then Give Them the Wheel

In exploring employee engagement in enterprise loyalty, we've unlocked experiences, unshackled employees, and loosened compensation to enable flexibility. In fact, my hope is that you're feeling free enough to release the tight controls on data, thereby giving frontline employees the access they need to deliver on your customer strategy.

Loyalty programs are great employee empowerment instruments. Take the Club Matas program, which was introduced in 2010 by the Danish skin care and cosmetics chain Matas. The program invites members to create online profiles or landing pages that are built around their specific preferences and interests. This information is then used to customize offers specific to that shopper, creating a straightforward value exchange. The customer's profile can also be accessed by employees, who can use it to make relevant product or service suggestions when the customer scans her card.

In 2011, Matas advanced its customer-employee connection by launching a mobile app that notifies users of every new product, event, or promotion. Through the app, users can search more than thirteen thousand beauty products and place favorites in a personal information filter called "my closet." Employees then send notifications when something important occurs with one of these products.[10]

Memberships numbers prove Matas is on the right track. In the program's first three months more than 16 percent of Danish women over eighteen joined the club.[11] By 2011 it had attracted almost seven hundred thousand members and earned a 2011 Direct Marketing Award.[12]

Similar to Club Matas, Safeway's Elite loyalty program is a practical example of a company providing its employees customer profile information that benefits both parties. The question is, where does this go, and what's the balance between pure-play technological features, such as digital check-ins and old-fashioned human contact, albeit enhanced by technology? With mobile innovations you could obtain permission from your customers to let you see when they are in proximity to your locations so you can provide them with better service and offers. True, it's not for everyone, but it eliminates the frustration of getting coupons after the shopping trip rather than before. If executed well, and if it's permission-based, it adds to customer value and convenience. The trick is putting that human face behind every technological interaction.

After all, while the visionaries may be in the corner offices, it's the frontline employees who are the eyes and ears of the organization. They scout the territory, witness the way consumers shop, observe what they bring into a dressing room and what they leave behind, and they hear specific product requests.

Naisten Pukutehdas, a women's clothing retailer in Finland, installed radio-frequency identification (RFID) sensors on its store shelves so that workers can get real-time inventory updates and automatic notices when it is time to replenish an item.[13] It also equipped its fitting rooms with wall-mounted smart screens that use RFID technology to read the tags of incoming items. This information is used to prompt the retrieval of related clothing and accessory images. When the shopper presses the screen to select items she would like to try with the garment, the screen displays them with product information, such as colors and sizes.

This is a great model of using operational mechanisms to enhance the store experience. But imagine if you could use this technology, in combination with data, in a way that inspires a relevant experience between the employee and the customer. The real potential value of such innovations, in terms of future relationship marketing and improved service opportunities, exists by connecting the information to the customer.

Such forward-leaning innovations supply employees with the tools to communicate what they see and hear up through the ranks. Such "listening posts" not only allow management to learn the nuances of customer preferences firsthand, they also provide employees the chance to share ideas on what would improve their lives on the job, and I'm not just talking free coffee and doughnuts. Properly recognized, your employees will equate job quality with their own performance and request the tools and information they need to optimize it.

All of which requires the most important leverage tool—communications.

CHAPTER 9

I Call, I Tweet—but How Do I Use Communications to Complete the Customer Experience?

The customer experience comes together at the moment a person is in your store, eating your food, checking into your hotel, sitting on your plane, surfing your Web site, or whenever else you directly interact with him or her. It's showtime. We've explored how data collection, targeting models, technology infrastructure, employee engagement, and relevance can deliver customer intimacy. When marketers combine these pieces, they reinforce customer choice, change customer behavior, and deliver winning customer experiences. The moment of truth occurs when the customer, who is time-starved, media inundated, overwhelmed with choice, and generally distracted, finally sees relevance in your messages and gives you his or her complete attention. This is the make-it-or-break-it moment for communications channels and messaging to come together in just the right measure to drive customer intimacy.

Say you are in the coach seat of a delayed flight: Wouldn't this be a great time for the carrier to reach out to you with a reassuring message? United Airlines thinks so. And so it happened one summer day, when a colleague at COLLOQUY boarded a 7:30 A.M. flight to catch an 11:00 A.M. meeting. Soon after taking her seat, surprise! Mechanical delays, and the United flight didn't even take off until 2:00 P.M. But being an experienced road warrior, she took the disruption in stride. These things happen. She pulled out her BlackBerry, relaxed, and made the best of it.

Still, let's take a moment to contemplate the preparation that goes into catching a 7:30 A.M. flight in a busy city. You are up at 4:00 A.M. after going to bed at 11:00 P.M. You leave your family before they awaken and you battle with traffic and parking. Then there's the shuttle, security, and the cramped aircraft. Only to miss that crucial meeting! You get the idea.

United also gets the idea. Instead of letting a planeload of business travelers, many of whom were United Mileage Plus members, beef about the inconvenience all the way to their final destinations, United headed the problem off before the snack cart arrived. When cell phones were powered up a "beep" sounded, and a text message from United was waiting:

> On behalf of all of us at United, I want to express my sincere apologies for the experience you had on Flight 3434 on June 13, 2011.
>
> At United, we take pride in being a reliable part of your travel plans. Your satisfaction and business mean a great deal to me. I would like to invite you to visit the following website to select a token of my appreciation.

The message was signed by Sherri Hermance, United Airlines Customer Care. Following the message was a link to an "appreciation" Web site where passengers could choose a meaningful makeup offer of either seven thousand Mileage Plus points, a dollar-based certificate, or a percentage-discount certificate.

Impressed and curious, my associate pondered the speed of United's apology and its befitting reward, and wondered if her frequent-flier status in the program made her one of the privileged few. So she asked a few other passengers if they had gotten a similar message. Sure enough, the other Mileage Plus members on the flight had also received a personal note from United.

Consider the effect of such a well-timed, resonant message. Instead of asking its top travelers to accept major delays as a normal part of business and risking days of grumbling from them, United had its passengers buzzing in the aisles for an entirely different, and positive, reason. United had reached out in a way that was timely and sincere, and with a gesture to compensate some passengers for the inconvenience they had suffered. It did so with an act of atonement that was of fair value, and by giving its members the choice of picking their gift. United didn't just say "I'm sorry"; it also provided a token of its appreciation.

By reaching out to its word-of-mouth champions, United reduced the likelihood that its best brand advocates would become "madvocates" who would tell a different story. Having the infrastructure in place to deliver a real-time triggered, service-recovery message, United was able to achieve maximum relevance. The outcome would have been very different had its apology arrived two days later. By then its passengers would have already spread the negative word.

Indeed, my associate blogged about her happy experience on United soon after it took place.[1] How's that for positive word-of-mouth communications?

Can We Talk? The Crux of Communications

This story captures in so many ways how a company can communicate effectively with its customers. It sounds simple, but the general rule of thumb is that the more straightforward the communications *seem* to the customer, the more complexity exists behind the scenes of contact management and marketing operations. To maintain sustainable customer engagement, through boom and lean times, you will want to invest in an ever-changing, multichannel network of relevant communications. This network will be the basis for managing customer relevance and risk. But like any other media, the communications framework is fragmented by multiple channels, customer segments, and technological capabilities. For starters, any worthwhile customer-management program will start with customer segments based on behavioral and attitudinal motivations, and then facilitate the creation of the optimal messaging for each. For example, say my wife and I were both invited to shop at lululemon this weekend, but my message involved power-wicking workout clothing while my wife's promoted yoga apparel. Same store, same household, but segmented messaging.

In addition to the expected communications via e-mail, direct mail, marketing, or social media, our personalized messages may also involve physical assets, such as store layout, product selection, or after-hours events.

But how do we ensure that the very capability that makes us more effective in building customer intimacy doesn't become a runaway train of dissonance? For the product obsessed and operational opportunists in the crowd, I'm going to take a page from the manufacturing sector. Think of communications like car assembly.

We're building a car, but not just any car. Imagine one that suits your brand. It could be the new Fiat Cinquecento for the functional commuter or the Porsche Panamera for the luxury driver. Regardless of the brand, the car must operate at peak performance with zero defects for us to call it an engineering triumph. Parts are brought in from around the world and around the corner. The grille, the radiator, the spoiler, the trim package, and the roof rack are all designed to perform very different functions, but they have a uniform purpose, which is to conform to the specifications of the car. But assemble the parts without a brilliantly engineered plan that enables these elements to work together in concert, or without a clear expectation of the end product's performance, and you end up with an AMC Pacer or, worse, a 1961 Chevy Corvair.[2]

And so it is with each element in your communications arsenal. Each component may be sufficient on its own, but when bound together by a common purpose, such as delivering a brand experience and customer intimacy, the combined effect has increased horsepower. And yet, that's not always how it feels.

Too often we see a call center with a one-size-fits-all approach to customer service while the marketing group is delivering communications based on value-based segments. You have a keen focus on customer data and campaign measurement, but you can't link your Web analytics to your direct marketing results. Organizational hierarchies and data ghettos across your company are a barrier to integrated communications, and you find yourself in a constant search for a unifying principle to sync this complex network of customer communications. But fear not. Just like with a car's assembly, you can start with a blueprint of the customer-management plan and all the parts designed to serve that vision. Remember, it's a good customer plan you're building, not a good communications plan. These parts serve to deliver a zero-defects customer experience, and your mission, if you choose to accept it, is to streamline the production and assembly of communications to align to that customer vision.

Communication Segmentation: Deconstruct to Reconstruct

Because not all customers look or act the same, experiential planning should start with three cuts of the customer stock. Value segmentation (who) helps us determine whom to target, based on a consumer's potential value, and how much we should invest in communications with this specific set of consumers. Solution segmentation (how) enables us to reach these high-value customers with messages that resonate. Last, impact segmentation (what) helps us identify the best offers and channels through which to deliver our communications.

Impact segmentation is at the heart of communications planning, and it's a moving target. Relevance depends on where the consumer is at a point in time, since location and immediate need affect how certain marketing messages will resonate.

Not surprisingly, some of the best examples of segmentation communications come from the grocery, pharmacy, and other high-frequency retail categories. They are the new power users of customer data because of the myriad of locational opportunities in the store—every product, aisle, and shelf is a communications opportunity.

Using an example at my own doorstep, there are the customized, one-to-one direct-mail pieces created by AIR MILES for our grocery and pharmacy clients, including the supermarket chains

Sobeys and Foodland. These inserts are highly personalized offers based on members' specific purchasing behavior and the store locations where each customer shops.

The coupons are created from a bank of hundreds of different offers and matched with individual shoppers using behavior modeling. This is relevancy in action—of the million pieces that are mailed, 987,000 are unique. The package includes: a letter from the local store manager, with a photo; a special offer to earn up to fifty dollars in groceries, free; and an insert of up to twelve customized product offers and coupons. The best part: The reward is tailored for each customer based on his or her spending patterns, current and potential value, and whether he or she responds better to cash- or points-based rewards.

Then, to make sure we reach all of Sobeys's and Foodland's customers through their medium of choice, the communications are integrated across channels, spanning direct mail, e-mail, and Web site landing pages. As mobile communications gain more active users in North America, they'll go there too.

These programs are enormously successful, with double-digit consumer response rates, and in a recent case a 66 percent increase in promotional recalls, an almost 37 percent unique open rate for Sobeys's e-mail, and a 26 percent e-mail click-through rate.

The Customer Is Job 1

Targeted communications programs are successful because they start with customer attributes determined through segmentation rather than with the annual channel plan, which is the usual way in most organizations. How many marketers start their annual budget planning with millions of dollars doled out to each of the

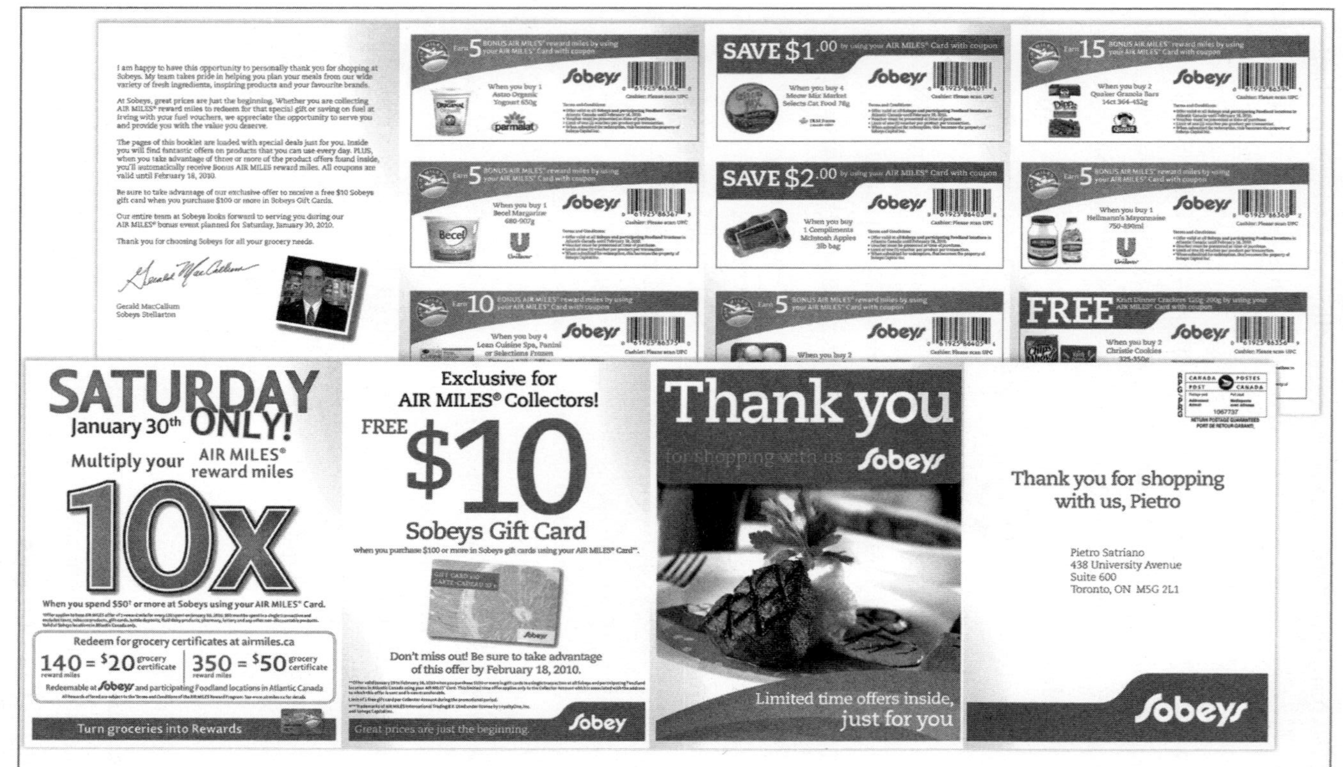

Source: LoyaltyOne

Each insert was customized based on the specific customer's purchasing habits.

functional communications groups? How often have we heard: "Here's $15 million for TV and another $15 million for direct marketing, and the Web site gets the balance . . . spread it across all customers as you see fit." Then a dutiful team further subdivides the pie and allocates to initiatives, with a nod to all the core marketing strategies that came out of the annual planning process. Finally, at the final stages, the team lines up customer segments against the plan to make sure no one is left out.

The reality is that companies define strategy as point solutions, isolating these functions when they need to be fully integrated and considered a part of everyone's mandate. The mystery of social media is, for many companies, a perfect example of this phenomenon. Rather than recognizing the foundational shift in how consumers interact with brands and companies, many organizations have taken old-world methods from mass media and tried to translate them for a new-world reality. They're strategizing communications vehicles and offers before even considering the customer and the purpose of the channel, a process I can only describe as "ready, fire, aim."

Turning the traditional marketing planning process on its head will likely result in budget reallocation, but could also identify unexpected savings. We made this shift at AIR MILES almost a decade ago and were able to redirect our investment from low-potential customers to high-potential ones, simply by identifying those whose behavior was least likely to change regardless of the communications. That's customer ROI management in a nutshell.

After all, your communications strategy is not simply the sum of its parts—e-mail, direct mail, tweets, texts, and in-store promotions—it is actually the *whole* of its parts. None of these channels on its own is a solution.

To me, mastering effective consumer communications comes down to the same principles as automotive design.[3] In fact, many similarities exist between the practice of aerodynamics, ergonomics, and modeling, and the processes required to build customer marketing. Each involves designing for the human form and human behavior, and both involve analytical methods governed by trial and error, constant improvement, and adaptation.

Communications Design: The Foundational Blueprint

We need to lay some critical ground rules if we're ever to achieve the traction we desire. First off, to fully understand our valued customers, we should combine our active listening with the ongoing analysis of data. There are three critical inputs for your communications design blueprint:

1. a longitudinal view of customer data
2. the ability to operate and respond in real time
3. the ability to integrate new media channels

Does Longitudinal Mean Lying Down?

To gain a longitudinal view of your data you'll want to move beyond traditional research snapshots of your customers, which are anchored in point-in-time activity, and observe customers through the data you obtain on them as their experience with you evolves. Think of it as the difference between first seeing a still photograph of your golf swing and then a video of it. One shows it frozen in time, the other shows its course, so that you can determine, as in my case, the point of failure. You essentially have to track that customer's behavior from acquisition to activation to increased spending to the purchase of ancillary products, and so on down the line. Again, this is an area where your marketing structure may fail you. If you think about traditional telecommunications and credit card marketing departments, the acquisition group is only responsible for getting the customer to activate his or her account, then that customer is handed off to the retention group. Connecting the dots on customer data is critical to making great customer communications work, often by advising on what to say or do during real-time customer interactions.

As Gartner Inc., the technology research and advisory company, outlines in its discussion about marketing automation vendors, multichannel campaign management based on individual customer interactions is within reach of companies willing to deploy the necessary technologies.[4] What's missing is marketers' changed attitudes about adopting a longitudinal view of customer activity and putting one into practice. Customers are dynamic, and as their behavior changes they have unrecognized needs. Keeping abreast of those needs requires that our marketing approaches identify relationships, not just moments in time, so that we can more genuinely realize each customer's values and preferences both today and as they change.

This is especially the case when it comes to your "next-best" customers, who can represent more opportunity than your best customers, since your best customers are already giving you most, if not all, of their business. But consider this fact: Very few of the top 20 percent of your customers are 100 percent loyal to your brand alone. You're probably getting most of their spending, but certainly not all. You needn't take my word for it. Take twenty-five of your loyal customers out to dinner and you'll soon discover the lost opportunities. Even if they're spending just 5 percent less than they could be, what would that add up to? Is it in the thousands or in the millions?

Contrary to what you might think, increasing engagement with these customers may not require further price cuts, but instead entail value-added services and benefits.

The telecommunications business is notorious for price discounting and other margin-cutting tactics to win customer loyalty, but some industry leaders have taken a different tack. Case in point: Turkey's Turkcell puts considerable muscle behind delivering unexpected rewards designed to captivate its customers, such as free theater tickets. Further, Turkcell has been able to build existing customer relationships by using its program data to pinpoint a segment of customers who do not appear to be very valuable but who were actually generating considerable business by having others call or text them frequently.[5]

By focusing on how to better serve these customers and retain and grow their business over the long run we can realize a superior brand experience and, in turn, may redirect customers from the discount mind-set.

Responding in Real Time? But What if I'm Speechless?

Let's face it: Despite all of the whiz-bang triggered communications and event-based marketing capabilities that have proliferated over the last ten years, the real power exists not in the delivery system but in how the company's customer data informs the message. All the e-mails in the world won't hit their mark if they are geared to sell a tall man's suit to a jockey.

Without the beginnings of a rich customer-data asset, and the ability to collect, store, and share it over time, your messages will come up short. But not all data fits nicely into databases. Unstructured data—textual information from customers that often arrives though social interactions—could include notes taken by a call center representative regarding questions or issues. With the immense popularity of social media, including Facebook, Twitter, blogs, and even texts, this data is expected to grow at almost three times the rate of the transactional information in your database.[6]

Harnessing this dialogue will be key to growing customer intimacy, since social communications provide an unscripted opportunity to capture and respond to candid comments—again, in real time. And count yourself lucky if you're invited to the party, since more than 80 percent of consumers say they follow only five or fewer brands online, according to Cone's 2010 Consumer New Media Study.[7]

Yet by 2012, 65 percent of service interactions are expected to take place online,[8] so your customers are either talking with you or they are talking behind your back. The good news is that the dialogue is also occurring across most companies, to the point where the PR, marketing, and customer-care departments are vying to "own" the social media channel. But the ownership question is really a distraction. The missed opportunity is in figuring out the right things to say, how to interpret what you're hearing, and mining the information for new insights.

How Do I Sell Myself Without Making It All About Me?

As my friend Mitch Joel, the president of Twist Image and author of *Six Pixels of Separation*, recently put it: Social media is not a medium, it is its own platform. Anyone can post anything and share it for free, and in a way that removes the gatekeepers.

For this reason your content should be as findable and shareable as possible—and it should not be all about yourself, he said.

"Ninety percent of the brands that make you yawn on social media channels are completely narcissistic in their approach," Mitch told me. "We have a world where content is really just thinly veiled marketing pap. Brands fail at social media because in a world of publishing content, they are still just marketers."

In his view, in fact, when it comes to understanding and researching products, consumers are actually ahead of marketers for the first time in history, thanks to digital technology. This, combined with social media's fluid and open nature, can make for a tricky exchange. Consumers have varying opinions about what a brand should and should not do, and these preferences may fluctuate from brand to brand, Mitch said. The kick in the head is that there is no defined formula. What works for Starbucks might not work for Caribou Coffee, and what works for the European fashion chain H&M might not work for the service-focused Nordstrom.

Brands may find real humility in the social space. You know right away how many people are following and responding to you, and in what context. Social media shines a light on brands—positive, negative, and neutral, so be prepared.

"Social media is an opportunity for businesses to have a direct relationship with their consumers, and it's scalable," Mitch told me, as we wrapped up our conversation. "The brands that struggle are those who are not active on the social media spheres, because when a crisis or complaint does erupt, it is challenging to have a positive resolution if they're not somewhat active and responsive to their consumers on the platforms that those consumers are using to express themselves."

Sounds Like a Runaway Train

I would liken the explosion of social media to the possibilities presented when we advanced to 4G from 2G networks. It is changing our two-way, customer-to-company conversations into out in the open trialogues, wherein customers can enter into a dialogue not only with the brand but also with each other. As Mitch pointed out, these relationships are scalable, so be sure your message is authentic and of value.

One instance of a company creating and leading a trialogue is the consumer electronics chain Best Buy, whose Twelpforce of more than twenty-two hundred employees volunteer to answer questions tweeted by Best Buy Twitter followers.[9]

Or, for a company that has established a real link between communications and rewards, there's KLM Royal Dutch Airlines. Through its KLM Surprise program, piloted in 2010, the carrier recognized select passengers with customized gifts stemming from information they had shared on Twitter, Facebook, and other social networks. One of its guests, who had mentioned his upcoming birthday, received a glass of champagne. Another, who while in New York lamented that he wouldn't be able to watch his favorite soccer team play its biggest game of the year, received a New York guidebook that highlighted pubs and bars that aired the games.[10] Nice surprise, nice word of mouth.

If there is any doubt about the value of such trialogues, consider these numbers: Facebook fans spend on average almost $72 more on the products they follow than those who are not fans, according to a June 2010 survey of four thousand people by Syncapse and Hotspex Market Research. Further, fans are 41 percent more likely than nonfans to recommend that product to friends, while 28 percent are more likely to continue using the brand.[11]

Having a longitudinal data view of the consumer, managing real-time messaging, and engaging in social media are decisive steps in shaping customer communications. The operational capabilities will come with continued investment over time, but the turning point will be the attitudinal shift you motivate within the organization. Getting channel marketers to think like customer marketers will not happen overnight.

Transference, or the Art of Copying Shamelessly

But few things worth working for do occur overnight. It's a little-known fact, for instance, that the science of aerodynamics was inspired by biology, and that the sleek, teardrop design came from observing the swimming movement of fish.[12] And so it is that we need to look afield to find our marketing inspiration and extend the expectations of the customer to industries beyond our own.

What I mean is that companies tend to compare themselves with others in the same industry. We are all guilty of myopic business practices and me-too marketing: Airlines measure themselves against other carriers, and credit card companies copy other card lenders. Retailers change their return policy when their competitors do, and cell phone carriers wait for their rivals to offer free texting before doing the same. But consumers don't frame their experiences in the same way. They transfer their expectations from one brand or industry to another: "I get special check-in treatment for being a frequent flier, so why can't I get the same treatment as a season ticket holder and have access to a special concessions line?" (If that means premium hot dogs, then I'm all for it.) Companies frame their communications programs around how their consumers perceive and respond to their brand, but consumers compare individual experiences against the multitude of interactions they have all day.

You can apply transference of experience when setting out to segment your customers by preferences, activities, and communications methods. What other kinds of services or merchants are they likely to frequent, and what are the talked-about offers or perks in these industries?

Customer-First Assembly: Communications in Reverse

Once the company has opened its strategizing to include transference it will find that it has richer resources to approach communications with the customer first. But if communications are begun in low gear, with channel and vehicle strategies, and then are worked up to align with customer segments, and ultimately to calibrate to business goals, then it's time to shift your vehicle into reverse.

In customer-first assembly you start with a customer goal—a 15 percent lift in the frequency of purchasing among your next-best customers, a 5 percent increase in coupon redemption, or maybe a 2 percent lift in your credit card activation rate. Next you align your communications investments by segment—we'll invest heavily in the youth segment with high cross-shop potential and earmark 20 percent of the budget to keeping our best customers humming along at their optimum performance. Then, and only then, do you start communications planning by identifying the best channel for reaching specific groups of consumers at different times and in different circumstances.

For help, draw on those advanced marketing algorithms that will cross-reference all of the data to provide swift solutions to consumer needs. With this information, the offering can be delivered through a communications method that resonates with the consumer, effectively closing the loop.

Take the case of Indigo Books, the largest bookstore chain in Canada. Faced with increased economic uncertainty, combined with the proliferation of electronic tablets, Indigo sought a way to engage its most active members and make them feel like they were well taken care of, not just at the point of purchase, but on an ongoing basis. Through its Premier Silver Promo Pack the bookstore chain developed a product recommendation algorithm that uses customer preferences, behavior, and transactional data to identify books and products that would interest the customer.

Through segmentation, Indigo created a platform for automated e-mail distribution for on-demand recommendations across channels, from its Web site to store kiosks. The results beat expectations, with a 47 percent increase in open rates and a 71 percent increase in incremental revenue over the control group.[13]

Starting with a customer-first communications strategy is the true foundation for marketing ROI. The current and potential value of your customers is the basis for deciding on channel investments and the communications plan. This starting point helps shape the content and context of your messaging, the most effective channels for each message's delivery, and the performance measures to quantify effectiveness.

And the company will typically be measuring against several channels. The successful execution of multichannel communications strategies requires the ability to break away from a one-way advertising environment and take on multiple discussions through the integration of all mediums. View social, digital, and mobile strategies as integral parts of everything the company does with the consumer. Doing so requires consistency across channels. A customer shouldn't receive an offer for petite clothing in her e-mail and for large-sized clothing through a direct-mail catalog. The only message this communicates is that the company does not know her.

This Triggers a Thought . . .

That takes care of proactive communications, but the company will also need to set aside a budget for reactive communications or triggered marketing, those event-prompted messages that can range from a birthday discount to a mailed notice that the customer's gift card still carries a balance. There are in fact two ways to execute triggered marketing. The first method involves planning communications and offers by segment, and the second is to plan by activity. Triggered communications work very well when started by event (new car purchase) and then tailored by segment at the time of the trigger (single up-and-comer, age twenty-five). The messaging will need to be contextually relevant, but timing is everything, so unless the company is exceptionally quick in its marketing execution, automation is the only reasonable way to execute.

Such automated programs can markedly enhance the way a company's customers view its services, especially when the strategy is designed with the goal of customer engagement. Take the classic example of follow-up surveys. OpenTable, the online restaurant reservation site, sends quick surveys to its dining members, and the responses feed its system. Responsible cell phone service providers alert customers if they are approaching their minutes limit. And I have a friend whose BMW sends her e-mails when it's time for regular maintenance.

Then there is wellQ, a service we developed with the American Pharmacists Association to improve prescription fulfillment by automatically messaging patients with daily medication reminders. WellQ supplements its customized reminders with a secure Web page that offers health tips, tools, and practical lifestyle resources. In an internal 2010 study among three hundred U.S. patients, those who used wellQ showed a 13.3 percent increase in prescription adherence. Most significant, those patients least likely to stick to their drug regimen improved their adherence by 65 percent.

Once I Have a Trusted Message, Then More Is Better, Right?

These are great communications programs, yet there are times when the messenger does need to be set straight. The relative affordability of digital communications such as e-mail and texts has led to a tendency to abuse the privilege. A company needs to balance the ease of e-mail communications against respect for the customer, because it can be a pretty fine line between e-mail acceptance and in-box madness. What is too much of a good thing? Use the "average man" test. Would the average man or woman expect to be contacted weekly with the status of his or her tire pressure? I don't think so.

And while we're on the subject, here's my other best advice: If you're not creating value, then don't send it. Just because you know your customers' addresses doesn't mean you've been invited to cram their mailboxes with crap. At least in a paper world there was a defined cost and timeline required to send someone a mailing. If we apply the same disciplined thinking to digital channels that we applied to traditional paper channels, in which there are genuine cost implications to overcommunicating, then the messaging would be that much more considered.

After all, each channel serves its own role. We know that a text message will typically be picked up within hours, while an e-mail may take days. Use your channels appropriately. Count on texts for time-sensitive, time-limited offers and on e-mail for deeper communications that are less reliant on a schedule or drop date.

Finally, be sure to have a proper measurement practice in place to account for all of your communications efforts: listen, track, engage, and respond.

Let's look again at social media. While many companies are throwing themselves into the social fray, very few employ a clear measure of success. A full 65 percent of companies do not use listening tools to track what their customers are saying about their brands online, according to a 2010 study by COLLOQUY and the Direct Marketing Association.[14]

Too often organizations execute targeted communications

with their clients and then, in an effort to get the highest response, opt to exclude measurement control cells. Wrong, wrong, wrong. Measured marketing means operating in a test-and-learn environment. The key to systematic communications efficiency over time is knowing what works and what doesn't, the relative return on investment, and the ability to repeat the elements that are most successful while abandoning those that aren't.

But if It Breaks, Fix It

The other beauty of measured marketing is that it affords us a blueprint to our mistakes. Turn that blueprint over, and the solution can be found.

In fact, I dare you to be prepared to fail. How else will you learn your limitations? Today's technology, through data collection, algorithms, real-time purchase tracking, and geo-tracking, is a communications enabler of unprecedented strength, yet we are not fully leveraging the capabilities that are available to us as marketers. Does doing so add complexity? You bet it does. Can it create incremental profit? Absolutely. Will everything work? Surely not. But if you don't measure it, you won't know where the system broke down, or where to focus the company's attention.

A company's success, meantime, will likewise be measured by its ability to deliver communications that are:

- personalized to reflect what the customer has shared, but are not prying;
- multichannel based on need and relevancy;
- consistent, reflecting meaningful integration of messaging between channels;

- nimble enough to seize the moment when the customer is tuned in;
- respectful, because after all, it's a relationship, not a one-night stand.

It's OK to Keep Some Customer Information a Secret

The methods a company relies on to gather and use customer information can dramatically enhance the customer experience and build equity over time. If you believe that relevant communications engender higher brand reputation and loyalty, then you have to recognize that how you enforce and practice safe data collection could be a critical differentiator for your company.

It's a virtuous cycle. The responsible management of information and appropriate, nonabusive use of data will result in the customer's increasing willingness to provide additional and potentially more insightful information. And then back through the cycle it goes, creating a greater competitive advantage with every rotation. Given the nature of this cycle, understanding how to operate within the privacy guardrails is critical to success.

In the end, of all the issues facing marketers today, the one attracting the most attention is the ongoing debate between the marketer's hunger to obtain more customer information and the public's desire for transparency and security. Navigating the tightrope between these differing points of view requires balance, but through it you will achieve the conviction to make that loyalty leap.

CHAPTER 10

How Do We Take the "Pry" Out of Privacy?

In the spring of 2011, over the span of just a few months, more than one hundred million people woke up to learn that their personal information had been breached or compromised. By June such recognized names as Sony, Citigroup, NASA, the FBI, and the cryptography firm RSA were among the victims of such incidents or breaches. By midyear, 2011 was on track to be the worst year ever for these types of occurrences.

The headlines—as well as the brazen acts—were startling, and they inflamed concerns about privacy among consumers, particularly regarding how companies collected, stored, protected, and ultimately used their personal information. It didn't matter much that to some, data security and data privacy are actually separate though overlapping issues. When people's personal information is stolen or exposed there is a feeling that their privacy has been violated, and I can appreciate that feeling.

In fact, one third of American and Canadian consumers told us they have been alerted of a compromise of their personal information, and of them, 43 percent say they have been negatively affected.[1]

The strange part of all of this is that, from where I sit as a marketer, these events converge to form diametrically conflicting perspectives. From a marketer's standpoint I believe that the issue of data security is entirely separate and distinct from consumer privacy. Hackers and criminal activity have little to do with our job as stewards of consumer information. The former is an issue of security and safety, while the latter regards how we use data responsibly to benefit the customer.

The consumer, however, does not distinguish between data security and privacy. If someone receives a letter or e-mail telling him that his personal information has been compromised, all he cares about is the potential damage. So while data protection and regulation are a real industry consideration these days, my first priority as a marketer is managing how consumers will perceive either situation.

So here we are, trying to wear both hats.

In fact, I sympathize with consumers. Twice in the past twenty years we at LoyaltyOne have found ourselves the target of hackers seeking to steal information about our Collectors. In each case we saw evidence that these highly motivated computer criminals found value in plain old contact information. We needed to act fast.

In the most recent case, in 2011, our first action was to make sure our potentially affected e-mail-able AIR MILES Collectors were contacted. We advised them that there was a risk that their e-mail address information may have been compromised, and immediately followed up with advice on what they should do and what they should watch out for, such as e-mails from unknown sources. We did all we could to clarify the incident from a security perspective by highlighting the potential threats, including spam, in notices that we sent to our AIR MILES Collectors:

> We want you to be cautious when opening links or attachments from unknown third parties. We want to remind you that AIR MILES will never ask for your personal information or login credentials in an e-mail. As always, be cautious if you receive e-mails asking for your personal information and be on the lookout for unwanted spam. It is not our practice to request personal information by e-mail. As a reminder, we recommend that you:
>
> - Don't give your AIR MILES Collector number or PIN in e-mail
> - Don't respond to e-mails that require you to enter personal information directly into the e-mail
> - Don't respond to e-mails threatening to close your account if you do not take the immediate action of providing personal information
> - Don't reply to e-mails asking you to send personal information
>
> We regret that this has taken place and apologize if this causes you any inconvenience. We take your privacy very seriously and we will continue to work diligently to protect your personal information.

Our AIR MILES stakeholders reacted pragmatically. While I was deeply concerned that our client relationships were in jeopardy, I was heartened by the response of our partners, the AIR MILES sponsors, who represent some of the biggest brands in Canada. Together we had everything to lose with customer trust at stake, but their collective response was empathetic and eminently sensible. I have to say, if there ever was a time when the fabric of a data-oriented business was tested, this was it. Overwhelmingly, they understood that we had taken reasonable precautions against this sort of activity and said they understood that this was an extraordinary situation. What they really wanted to know was what we were doing to fix the situation and to prevent it from happening again. Otherwise, they were ready to return to our channels right away and continue using them.

Meanwhile, the reaction from our AIR MILES Collectors, or consumers, was negligible. This turned into one of those moments when all of the trust we had built and embedded over the years, through AIR MILES, had paid off in dividends. We received very few calls and noted very little activity or discussion through our social media monitoring. When we briefly halted our e-mail activity because of the incident, and then phased it back in slowly, we saw that our open and response rates had been unaffected. Even when some Collectors raised the issue on Facebook, others were the first to rise to our defense, responding with assurances that we had taken all the proper protective steps and reinforcing the fact that the issue was beyond our control. It was a test of our relationships, and rather than generating "madvocates," we discovered a strong base of brand advocates.

For this I certainly credit my team's proactivity in responding to the incident. They sprung into action with a thoughtful plan, recognizing that at a time like this trust takes center stage. I credit the trust we nurture with our Collectors. I believe this bank of goodwill has been built brick by brick, over time, through the consistent approach we take to safeguard and respect our customers' information. And it was there when we needed it most.

All of that said, we are not so proud as to not have learned from these experiences. For one thing, I felt the profound need to be timely and responsive. As soon as we were made aware of the issue, we scoped out the extent of it, lined up our action plan, and acted on it. One extra hour could have spelled the difference between years of acquired trust and a lost reputation. Our own research shows that 79 percent of American and Canadian consumers believe they should be notified of a breach within twenty-four hours, which is generally less time than what is being proposed or has already been enacted in many jurisdictions around the globe.[2]

Today we feel that we not only survived the data compromise, but also that we emerged from the challenge stronger than before, because we learned just how much our customers value their relationships with us. And we know, with abundant clarity, that all marketers face a variety of privacy-related pitfalls in collecting and using customer data. But there's a flip side to this story, and that is the role of responsibility in setting you apart from others in the industry.

We believe there are five basic principles for using data responsibly to create real value for the customer. They are:

1. Be transparent and reasonable
2. Be permission-based
3. Respect and protect data
4. Don't wear out the consumer's trust
5. Win-win is always better than win-lose

Before I elaborate further, it's useful to specify what I mean when I refer to information that needs to be safeguarded for customer privacy. There are really three kinds of customer data to consider:

- **purchase information:** This is basic transactional information shared as a by-product of the consumer's trust. The consumer is saying "Sure, since I do business with you, I am willing to enter into some form of data sharing with you as well." These transactions occur only because of the commercial nature of the relationship and include most of the traditional purchasing basics—what consumers buy, where they buy, and how often they buy.
- **declarative information:** This includes the basic customer information, such as name, address, and e-mail address, that a company needs in order to enter into a consumer (not commercial) relationship. Contact data is the minimal requirement, and it is a necessary condition for companies to create dialogue and an exchange of value. It happens every time a person hands over his or her loyalty card or device to the clerk. Consumers know that sharing this with a merchant means they are giving that company clearance to track what they are buying, which is a window into each of their worlds.
- **voluntary declarative information:** This is information that is not required for the relationship to exist, and therefore can be tricky. Companies may ask for such extended demographic or preference data, such as household income or number of children, but consumers may or may not want to share it. The

> response will likely depend on a correlation between what information is being requested and the consumer's understanding of why the company would want to acquire it. The onus is on the company to provide a valid reason for wanting this information and to provide a reasonable, reciprocal exchange of value.

It would be helpful to keep these levels of data in mind as we venture into the five essentials of using data responsibly; they will provide context and help to pose the right question when you ponder the reasonability of requests, or the value exchange thereof.

By now you're probably feeling the seriousness of the customer territory we've entered. I don't throw around words like responsibility, trust, and principles lightly, and I'm about to introduce a new word, "governance," to add gravity to the situation. So how did we get from the emotive ground of customer intimacy and loyalty to this solemn place?

I've relied on the stories of peers and on our own research to underscore why we need to get close to the consumer and how loyalty initiatives are among the greatest tools for enabling that relationship. And together we've explored how to use customer data throughout the entire enterprise, from the corner office to the front lines.

If you are truly serious about and committed to customer intimacy, then you will embrace these principles and honor them like they are your own P&L statement. In fact, let's think of them as our "privacy & loyalty" statement. If you want to be successful in turning customer information into customer intimacy, then P&L needs to represent both your financials and your privacy and loyalty measures, because how you handle your customers' data will directly affect your ability to outperform your competition.

Now that we've sobered up the data discussion, let's look at what's under the hood on this data governance pact.

1. Be transparent and reasonable

It's as clear as the blue skies in wintertime: The more transparent you are, the more engaged your customers will be. They will understand, in very simple language, what you are trying to do, what you're achieving, what's in it for them, and what's not in it for them.

The catch is that consumers and businesses don't always agree on the degrees of transparency. My yardstick goes back to the reasonable man test: what an average person would consider reasonable. OK then, so what is reasonable? That is hard to define, so let's apply U.S. Supreme Court Justice Potter Stewart's definition of pornography: We know it when we see it.

For example, say you are returning something to a local merchant, and the salesclerk asks for your driver's license, or maybe your address or phone number. Most people would think this is unreasonable. Why on earth would the merchant need this information when the credit card used for the purchase should be all that is required? A reasonable person would think "You know, I'm not so sure I'm going to shop here again." And who'd blame him?

The more clear and upfront a company is about its marketing plans for the consumer's information, the more likely he will be OK with sharing greater amounts of it, because the reasonability quotient goes up. It's basically a paired relationship. The greater the transparency the better the ability of the consumer to assess the reasonability of your request.

Which leads to an important point in this discussion that we've covered before: Collect only the data you need, and use the data you collect. When a company is transparent about its use of data, it enters into a promise with its customers. It needs to deliver on that promise. As we've seen, collecting data without using it to benefit the customer can be annoying and alienating. If a hotel's frequent-guest program is going to ask me what kind of pillow I want, then it needs to go the extra mile and provide me with that kind of pillow. When a company is open with its customer about its motives, is transparent in its activities, makes a clear promise, and delivers on that promise, customers will not only tolerate data collection, they'll embrace it, because they will clearly see the benefits.

Consumers, governments, regulators, and interest groups advocate for transparent and reasonable approaches for good reasons. Meanwhile, a lot of businesses choose to be only somewhat clear, and still they want everything. That is not always reasonable.

2. Be permission-based

My position is unwavering: If you are going to run a value exchange–based relationship with consumers, then you need to gain their trust. And the best way to gain customer trust and commitment is by being permission-based, and by giving them the opportunity to choose whether they will share information with you.

You need this kind of opt-in commitment, combined with transparency and reasonable data collection, to elevate the consumer relationship to the kind of holistic level that delivers the highest quality of information. Such solid loyalty will of course result in stronger relationships, better profits, higher sales, and increased relevance.

This is not to say that there isn't an entire industry that exists in which people exchange data for the primary purpose of acquiring consumers on a targeted basis, such as in the case of online cookie operators. There is, and this industry is most likely going to continue to thrive for years to come. But it will exist in a different realm from companies like ours, which works with corporate partners to create enduring relationships and connects with consumers in ways that can be differentiated. In my heart and in my mind I know that permission-based marketing is the real route to a fuller exchange and a fuller value proposition.

In a Web environment, for example, we live with search engine optimization and ad targeting systems. These are not permission-based. But frankly, if these companies use the information they gather judiciously, and deliver promotions or advertisements geared toward my personal interests at the right time—not months after I conduct a specific search—I would probably find that a more enriching experience than one in which I was being plastered with way off-target ads for, say, skydiving when I'm interested in hiking. In fact, if the online industry evolves to the point that it is creating a more relevant experience based on the information that it gleans from the Web user's behavior, then consumers will be better off than if they were getting mass messaging, permission or no permission. If consumers feel the messages and interactions are more relevant, then they consider themselves well served.

And to be truthful, either system—permission-based or not—can work with responsible marketers using it. Both have the potential to add value for the consumer if the data is respected and targeted appropriately. However, the company will not achieve the full potential of either method unless it takes a longitudinal view of a customer's brand interactions and uses those insights as the basis to build incremental value and relevance. In other words, while it's better to target customers based on past purchasing activity, you do need to acquire the customer first.

The problems arise when marketers push the boundaries in an environment without an opt-in provision and cross the creepy barriers into ultrapersonal and inappropriate areas, such as health issues, finance, or sex. If you're a furniture-store owner and you genuinely want to build a relationship with a consumer who just purchased a couch, and you don't have an opt-in tick box, why not literally go to the consumer and ask if you could send her materials about future furniture sales or other products you think she may be interested in down the road?

But this argument only makes the case that data gathering, however achieved, can improve the customer *experience,* which is a start, but it does not mean you will cement loyalty and trust. If you really want to build longevity and depth around the relationship, the way to do it is to engage in a proactive, permission-based relationship between the consumer and the brand. Then you may be able to enhance your ability to collect discretionary information that is relevant to the experience.

The concern from many companies that don't use consent-based marketing is that it could cost them in terms of potential market penetration. But with AIR MILES we pursued a permission-based approach, and look: We've got a 99.99 percent opt-in from our coalition membership base of consumers to receive our marketing communications. That translates into only ten thousand consumers, out of 10 million, who choose not to receive promotional offers from us.

The reason is because we have operated by the same code and beliefs since our inception, and that is that permission-based marketing leads to honor and trust. Trust leads to strong relationships. Strong relationships lead to greater profitability. It's a virtuous cycle, a system that feeds itself when operated with the right strategic intent and transparency.

3. Respect and protect data

Of course, the wonderful treasure that is a consumer's trust carries much value and much responsibility. This goes beyond guarding data like it is a corporate asset. It also means respecting the data. Companies need to safeguard the information they collect diligently. Whether the system it operates is an opt-in or opt-out one, it should use the data only as directed and as is permissible, retain it only as long as needed, don't use it for secondary purposes, such as selling it to a third party without permission, and always, always, always destroy it with care.

Unfortunately, security breaches still take place on a regular basis. As I discussed, almost one third of American and Canadian consumers, 32 percent, say that they have been notified that their information has been stolen or compromised.

A lot of companies are hesitant to mention data breaches when they occur because they think it's going to impact their brand negatively. They fear that consumers will sue. This is understandable, and controllable. The best precaution is to keep only the data necessary to serve the customer and then take the proper steps to protect it to the point that only your associates who need it have access to the actual files. And by consumer data I mean the actual data files that are worth money to scammers and others on the black market, not the general purchasing insights that should be shared discreetly with frontline employees as coded offers. For instance, while Hilton Hotels may use its masked data to determine that a guest prefers a room with a king-size bed away from the elevator, our customer care folks at AIR MILES see only enough activity to serve them better, such as for problem solving.

Businesses need to consider what level of information should be provided to the associates in varied situations, and what information they should even hold onto themselves. Ask: Is there any reason to keep credit card information months after a consumer made a purchase? Is there any cause to hold on to location-based data after it has served our need? And make sure all of the available protection mechanisms are in place, from data security and collection limits to top-level encryptions and third-party audits.

For instance, according to a 2010 Federal Trade Commission report, Microsoft has called for data-security standards for cloud-computing services. And Google announced that it would use encryption by default for its e-mail service.[3]

As victims of hacking incidents ourselves, we are continuously updating our security systems, diligently monitoring all data activity, and fine-tuning our action plans.

Such precautions highlight the need to understand the vulnerability and potentially unknown lure of consumer data, and to structure the company's protection accordingly. If it's transparent, if it acts quickly, if it's frank about the breach, if it takes all the precautionary steps, then consumers will be forgiving. They will be reasonable and understand that the hackers are the bad guys, not you.

At the end of the day, the real question is this: If the company is hacked or breached, could it stand up to the scrutiny of the customers and say it did everything reasonable, given the sensitivity of the data, to protect it? Is the company 100 percent certain that it can be transparent about any such issues that might arise?

By standing before the judge and jury of the consumer, with a clear conscience, it has preserved its relationships.

4. Don't wear out the consumer's trust

We all get to a point where we feel worn out and overloaded from too much information. Our e-mail in-box is busting with unwanted spam from sunup to sundown. Most of it is never opened; it goes straight into the digital trash bin. But for many of us, the annoyance lingers. We all can name at least one company or brand that relentlessly contacts us every day with a message of no real value.

Ensure that your company is not adding to this burden by not abusing a person's name and contact information, and also by not abusing that consumer's permission. Remember, he or she owns that information and merely granted you the go-ahead to use it responsibly. There is an element of trust in that transaction, so respect it. Again ask yourself: Are your e-mails too frequent, considering the content? Are they relevant to the customer's needs and desires at the time they arrive? Do they offer real value?

For instance, I have a friend who, in passionate support of a presidential candidate, gave campaign organizers her cell phone number. Now she continues to get a text message almost every day from the Democratic Party—after the election. She is also on the national do-not-call list, along with almost 48 percent of all other American and Canadian consumers, and according to our research,[4] she does not know how to opt out. But the ability to opt out is beside the point—she gave the campaign organizers her number, and then they took advantage of it.

This is one kind of abuse. There are others. Among them, don't abuse a customer's permission by treading into inappropriate areas. When it comes to the tone and frequency of messaging, the company has to be mindful of the consumers' personal boundaries. If a supermarket operator suddenly registers that somebody is buying Depend adult diapers, don't start sending him or her e-mails every day that refer to an incontinence problem. It is a sensitive issue, and besides, the product may have been purchased for someone else.

There are real business reasons for heeding these words. If marketing efforts annoy customers, because they are too frequent, intrusive, or just not relevant, customers will tune them out even if not opting out. A few paragraphs back I mentioned that we all receive e-mails that we simply delete without opening. How many have you deleted so far today? Now consider what it would take for those marketing companies to get your interest back. Think about these questions and apply the answers to your own operations.

I can tell you that at AIR MILES we have limited our e-mails to just two per week per Collector, despite huge demand from our sponsor partners and the technological ability to bombard customers with much more. We carefully monitor opt-outs and open rates to see that they remain healthy. And when a campaign doesn't create the right level of resonance, we change our marketing approach and advise our partners on ways to improve their own value through relevance.

But improving one's value means delivering something of value to the customer as well.

5. Win-win is always better than win-lose

We're back to the basics here, folks. When it comes to data exchange, nothing is given for free. You are not on the Web searching Google or using Facebook for nothing; your activity, your searches, your likes and dislikes are being used to support revenue in some way.

Most consumers are willing to live with this. In fact, it appears that American and Canadian consumers generally have low expectations when it comes to what they should get in return for their information. In 2011 only 36 percent of two thousand American and Canadian consumers we surveyed said they expected preferential treatment or improved product selections in exchange for their personal information. Barely half, 49 percent, said they expected to receive tailored offers based on what they buy, and 54 percent said they anticipated improved customer service. Said another way, 46 percent of consumers don't even expect better service in return for their personal information.[5] What has discouraged them so?

This is a call to action. Despite our work, despite all the tailored messaging and promotions, consumers still do not understand that a value exchange should be made available. There's an opportunity for companies to distinguish themselves through the data that is being shared, and to turn their customer information into customer intimacy. Imagine the potential of being the first company to fully capitalize on what's possible through data. You could be the Apple of customer information! If Apple had never made usability and design the cornerstone of computers and musical devices, we would all be sentenced to the hell of trying to figure out how to use digital music, and Microsoft could have prevailed without moving to the Windows platform. God help us—we might still be using green screens, and the mouse would long be gathering dust in the archives of Xerox.

Part of the reason for the consumer disconnect may be because our efforts toward recognition, communications, and rewards simply do not resonate. But let's face it: These numbers also reflect a shortfall of effort or execution on the part of marketers. And don't assume that just because consumers have tolerated such lopsided arrangements thus far that they will continue to do so. Jaded consumers will either lose interest in the brand or eventually find a rival that delivers worthwhile rewards in return for their information.

And if an organization takes advantage of a person's information to the point that the relationship becomes abusive, as in the case of my friend who received too many texts, then the company runs the risk of being completely shut out, meaning the consumer will turn off the personal information valve altogether.

Customers have a tacit human expectation of reciprocity, after all, and they can detect when that expectation has been violated. Trying to cut corners and tricking customers will backfire, always. The company's tether—its umbilical cord to this wonderful source of information—is only as good as its ability to manage its own greedy use and leveraging of that personal information, as well as its organizational integrity, to focus on creating real value for the consumer. It's not about the product exchange, cash, points, coupons, or whatever. It is about something bigger than that, which is relevancy. The more relevant the communication, and the offer within, the more engaged the consumer will be. Now there's a mutual value exchange.

But let's do the math and look at the compounding value of that data over time, by taking a longitudinal view of the consumer and his or her commercial exchanges year in and year out. The more information the company can put into the pot, the longer it can maintain the strength of that relationship, and the more discretionary the information that customer is willing to share, the greater the company's ability to heighten the relevance of its marketing. And the greater its relevancy, the more secure its relationships with its customers.

Building these connections is a little like developing face-to-face relationships with other people. In the beginning, you share a little. When the other party demonstrates that he or she can be responsible with what you have shared, then you reveal a little more. Gradually the relationship deepens. Customers in general are very comfortable taking a crawl-walk-run approach to sharing information, and it's a sensible way for companies to proceed in data collection and use. As long as customer information is used to enhance the customer experience, taking small steps along the way can lead to big things.

If you believe in these causes and business philosophies, then ultimately you will easily be able to live by these principles. And you will be able to make privacy a nonissue in your environment and to your customers.

Just remember: Don't $%@# it up!

EPILOGUE

Capitalizing on Customer Information: Can We Afford to Ignore It?

Oscar Wilde once said, "It is a very sad thing that nowadays there is so little useless information." This has never been more true than in today's data-rich environment. I'm convinced there are trillions of megabytes of customer data in the world today, and yet the vast majority of it goes through its usable shelf life never analyzed, never optimized, and never leveraged. Like a can of deviled ham, it just sits there gathering dust. But customer information today has moved well beyond generating mailing lists and looking at demographic attributes. It's a specialist's skill that's needed to comprehend the power of regression models, make sense of digital and retail behaviors, tell a story with cognitive research, and understand when to use ethnographic studies instead of price optimization models.

Just like being a doctor is about having a scientific leaning and a bedside manner, customer management and loyalty is also a combination of hard and soft skills. It's that perfect mix of art and science, in which you need both a statistical mind-set and the ability to accept unstructured data, as well as highly developed interpretive skills. And although we're not facing life-and-death situations, I believe we can make a difference in people's everyday lives by becoming more relevant, and by reflecting their behaviors and interests in the actions we take as a business. I've also seen that making sense of it all, and putting the right content in the right context, can affect business performance positively.

The question is: Are we willing to think beyond the data, breaking down the data ghettos so the entire organization can capitalize on the customer information that exists within them? Interpreting the behavior of customers and finding the right way to engage them in today's world, via the ever-growing and complex existing channels, is certainly daunting. Whether you are a large multinational or a smaller local player, the fact is that consumer behavior is typically contradictory and unpredictable. The same customer who shops for Armani may also shop at Walmart. Customers can give their cell phone service provider the worst service scores of any retailer, and yet that provider will remain the market leader in the sector. Why people buy and how they navigate those purchase decisions is a topic we may never fully appreciate, despite years of analysis and research. What I do know is that although consumers' behaviors may be capricious, the profile information provided through their transactional histories is highly predictive, and there's a significant opportunity for most organizations to observe, learn from, and leverage that information to create an improved customer experience, regardless of the channel.

I have the opportunity to attend and speak at many conferences, and I'm struck by the consistency of what I see and hear. There have been a lot of occasions when companies present their advancing efforts in multichannel marketing and data analysis, but when you brush away the rhetoric, the ugly truth is hard to miss: Most are still using old-school analysis methodologies and suboptimizing the loyalty card data or customer information they have obtained.

I recently watched a presentation in which the executives of one of the world's biggest retailers explained how they were using market research to help redefine the store of the future. Yet they seemed to ignore the customer information that was available in the company's database. We're talking about years of detailed information obtained from more than fifty million of its loyalty card customers, and it had so far been relegated to a minor role in the process. I'm not suggesting that market research shouldn't play a role; I'm just pointing out how that customer information could have been used to create insights and decisions to support the design of its new customer experience. The best part of the presentation: The speaker admitted that his company would at some future time have to enter into an active dialogue with its customers, both virtually via its loyalty card and live in the store.

Indeed, one of my biggest fascinations is the loyalty marketing industry's preoccupation with how to optimize this new multichannel environment, and particularly the role of social media. After all, the world of communication is fundamentally a world governed by confusion. Granted, it's more complex than it's ever been, and there are more ways to spend that limited pool of marketing dollars. Marshall McLuhan, the author of *Understanding Media: The Extensions of Man,* is often quoted as saying, "The medium is the message."[1] What I think McLuhan was trying to communicate is that the advent of new channels, where consumers define and guide the conversation, has fundamentally changed the way the "message" is constructed. Defining a brand today is as much about how your customers engage in the brand conversation as it is about how you try to connect to consumers and shape their impressions of the brand. And yet, while innovations such as social media are changing the landscape, creating greater transparency and a need for more brand authenticity, the message is still the message. How we understand and interpret our customers' motivations, both attitudinal and behavioral, is critical to how we integrate today's plethora of marketing tools to help shape their experience with our brands.

It's like picking the right medical specialist for the task at hand. We need representatives from all disciplines to treat the whole person, and each has but one contributor. In the same way, social media or cell phone communications do not own the entire customer experience; instead, the combination of all customer touch points will define it. It's imperative to get the right combination of content and channel to create consistent interactions. Understanding how a customer interacts with a brand is the critical ingredient in getting the recipe right. Unfortunately, many marketing organizations are spending too much time worrying about the channel and a disproportionate amount on getting the content and context right when they should be mining their customer information.

The world is changing quickly, and yet many of the customer's core motivations remain highly correlated to what we have always thought of as important. While the consumer may appear complex and irrational, we are creatures of habit, and we respond best to things that resonate with who we are and what we've done before, as well as with the basic hopes and fears that are grounded in our limbic brain. We also are quick to build on positive and negative experiences and extend them to other interactions in our lives. This is of particular importance and supports a point that I still remember well from my first marketing course in business school:

"If you can't say anything about the product, then talk about the packaging."

It is challenging for many companies to differentiate themselves through the product. But even when it is not, why stop there? Why not consider even better ways to deliver that product to the customer? You may even find inspiration from beyond the traditional set of competitors that are used as comparatives. The opportunity exists to take a fearless step forward, leveraging the best customer intimacy practices of other industries and sectors to leapfrog the competition. Start with imagining what could be and then work backward. If some way can be found to personalize the experience, then the company will be on its way to using relevance to engender emotional loyalty, and ultimately the future value of all the purchases made by its customers.

My sincere hope is that the ideas presented in *The Loyalty Leap* will launch a new exploratory path for companies, and that they will take their first steps toward a customer-committed culture. Not just one in which the customer is placed first but one where the whole organization understands the value of customer information, one in which that information is set free across the organization to support the product experience and customer communications that together form a highly relevant experience for the customer. Consumers are underwhelmed by the way their information is being used today, and they will embrace those organizations that focus on recognizing their individual preferences and creating a relevant and compelling experience for them. Doing this requires a companywide commitment to taking that symbolic step.

The paradox of business today is that playing it safe may actually be the riskiest strategy of all.

APPENDIX A

Excuse Me, but Have We Met?

Wow, so you think you know someone.

We at LoyaltyOne did, anyway, until we saw the results of an extensive survey that reveals surprising attitudes and expectations about consumer privacy. We conducted a survey in 2011 of American and Canadian consumers to gauge how people feel about data collection and use. We also asked about privacy concerns, the measures people take to protect their identities, and the benefits they expect in return for sharing their personal information.

It turned out that despite decades of hard work to better understand consumers, to enable us to offer them more relevant services and values, roughly half of the population still does not expect any benefit at all. Only 49 percent of the two thousand survey respondents said they looked forward to tailored offers based on what they buy. Worse, 74 percent of responding consumers said they do not feel they receive any benefits at all from sharing their personal information.

These anemic expectations are driven by the experiences consumers have had in the marketplace. Hotel loyalty members repeatedly say they prefer a room away from the elevator but are then booked in one next door to it. A grocery shopper is a regular buyer of Crest yet gets coupons for Colgate. The cashier or desk clerk is more often than not oblivious to a customer's loyalty membership status, and the customer leaves feeling cheated by the experience.

How many of us can confidently say that all of our customers feel valued by us, and that they believe they receive a fair exchange of services or offers in return for their information? We have all of this wonderful information, yet somehow it is still not being to put work in a way that is relevant to our customers.

Now imagine what would happen if a rival company acts on that same customer information more effectively, and gets the message and the offer right.

These findings are a call to action. Consumers said they were generally suspicious of data marketing companies and were concerned about their personal privacy; still, our research shows that they did little to protect themselves and had limited awareness regarding what companies actually know about them. Many respondents said they were willing to share more personal information if it meant getting product or service offers, but at the same time they did not want to be profiled based on their income bracket or credit history.

Yes, it is a bit of a Gordian knot. But let's try to puzzle out the meaning of these results, which if nothing else reveal that we all have much more to learn about each other.

Privacy, Perks, and Other Pointers

In the 2009 movie *Up in the Air*, the lead character, played by George Clooney, spends his professional and personal life chasing loyalty points and miles. In return he gets bragging rights to free plane tickets, expedited check-ins, and personal greetings from people who have never met him.

In reality, most consumers—74 percent—feel they get no preferential treatment at all in return for their information. However, 64 percent said they would be willing to share additional personal information if companies sent them more relevant communications.

Among the most surprising findings of our research is that 88 percent of the respondents thought companies used personal information primarily to benefit the business. Only 52 percent believed a company's intention was to use the information to better serve the customer. And 85 percent said they were "often concerned" about how much of their personal information was being held by others.

Indeed, 32 percent of our survey respondents said they had been notified that their personal information had been stolen or compromised. Of them, 43 percent said they had been negatively affected.

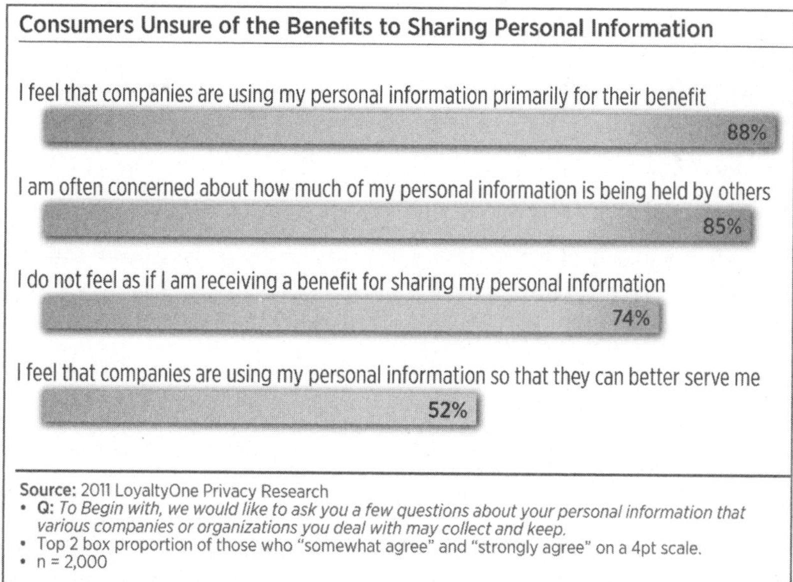

Source: 2011 LoyaltyOne Privacy Research
- **Q:** *To Begin with, we would like to ask you a few questions about your personal information that various companies or organizations you deal with may collect and keep.*
- Top 2 box proportion of those who "somewhat agree" and "strongly agree" on a 4pt scale.
- n = 2,000

Yet few consumers are proactive when it comes to taking measures to protect their privacy. Only 22 percent of survey respondents said they "always" read the fine print, meaning the privacy statements, contracts, or terms that come with their agreement to share personal information. Another 30 percent said they "often" do.

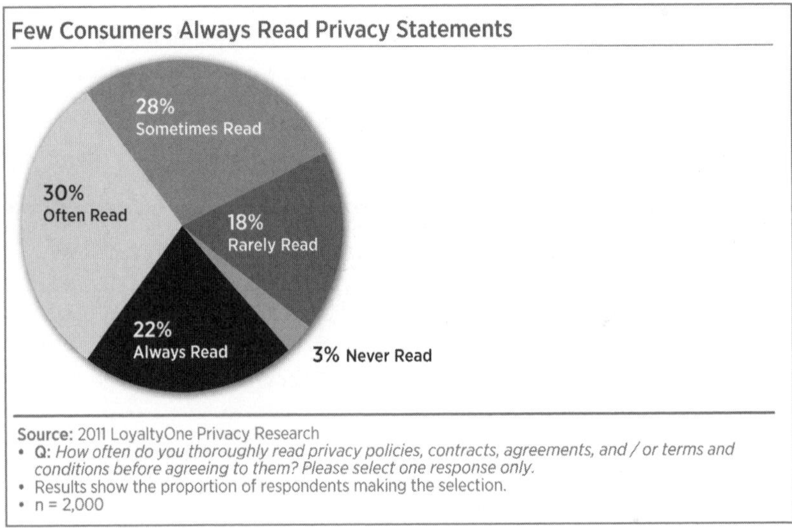

Few Consumers Always Read Privacy Statements

Source: 2011 LoyaltyOne Privacy Research
- **Q:** *How often do you thoroughly read privacy policies, contracts, agreements, and / or terms and conditions before agreeing to them? Please select one response only.*
- Results show the proportion of respondents making the selection.
- n = 2,000

Of the consumers we surveyed, 27 percent said they had in the previous twelve months deleted information from a social network, such as Facebook or Twitter, while 12 percent deleted their entire profile. And not even half of the respondents—48 percent—had registered on a do-not-call list.

If you think operating a loyalty program will earn you higher consumer awareness, then you're in for disappointment. Only 53 percent of respondents thought their loyalty program operators understood what they bought, while 48 percent thought their loyalty program kept a record of their shopping and entertainment habits, such as where they shopped. Of those using their loyalty card, 52 percent said they were concerned about their behavior being tracked.

So much for all of our hard work.

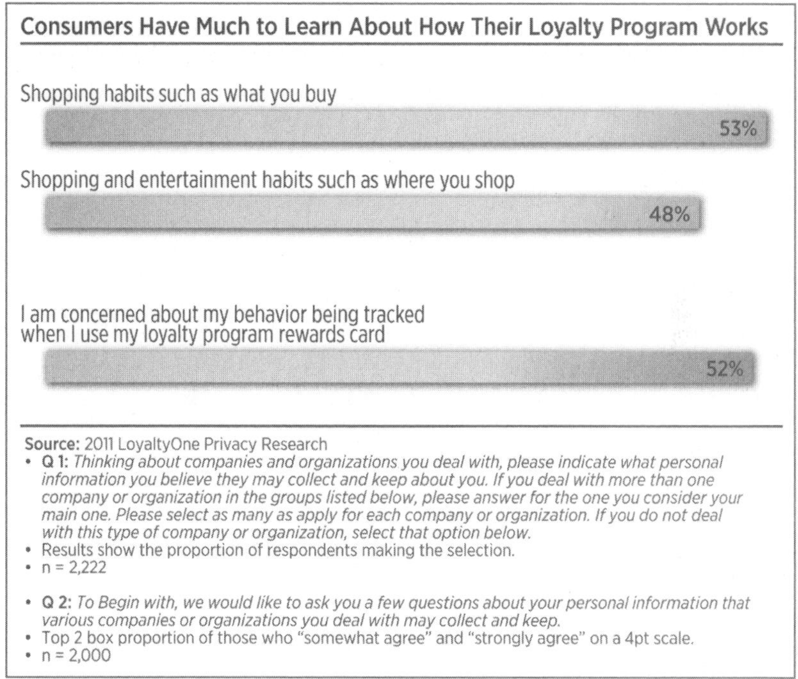

Coupons for Nothing, Chocolate for Free

So what do consumers want, and what should they expect from us? Well, we've learned that people generally like to get products for free, but they do not like shilling. For instance, almost 79 percent of consumers would welcome getting chocolate from a hotel chain if they had previously mentioned their favorite brand to a concierge in another chain location. And about 76 percent said it was acceptable for a diaper manufacturer to mail free samples to their home after a baby is born.

But fewer than half of the respondents thought it was acceptable for their credit card company to share their home renovation information with a retailer, even if it resulted in an offer for discounts on a home appliance. And just 31 percent said it was acceptable for a fuel chain to look up their address on a mailing list, find the average income of their neighborhood household, and then send offers for premium gas to higher-income residents and discounts for lower-grade gas to residents who earned less.

So what do consumers expect from us? Not much, sadly. While 71 percent of our survey respondents said they anticipated some sort of product discount in return for their personal information, just 54 percent expected improved service. Forty-one percent expect to get communications based on their preferences.

Only one third looked forward to additional information on products they had purchased or should purchase. This is despite one of the

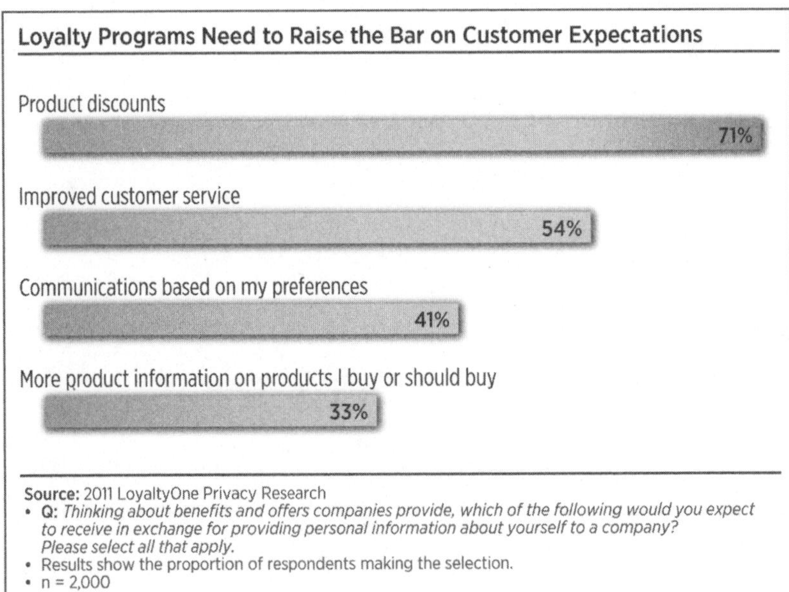

core purposes of a loyalty initiative—to match consumers with services and goods that will improve their lives.

What Are We to Do?

The declaration is clear. We need to bridge the gap between meeting the unique needs of our customers and building loyalty and trust. Doing this means knowing our customers better, not simply by gathering information that reflects their purchasing behavior, but by pulling the meaning from it. I suggest these action items:

1. **Invest in reaching the members you have.** Our consumers lead complex lives, so we need to reach them in multiple ways. A good method for doing so is by investing in multifaceted communications strategies that optimize the variety of channels we use. Such communications include social media, which can foster word-of-mouth growth, rather than the massive membership enrollment drives of years past.

2. **Create new value propositions.** Look, if people do not recognize their rewards it is because the rewards we are offering just do not resonate. We need to become creative and expand our recognition options to meet the advancing lifestyles of consumers. This could range from coalitions—partnering with other merchants to expand reward choices—to aligning with nonprofits or other causes. The trick is to move beyond basic discounts and other simple frills and extend our recognition offers to reflect all the things a consumer might value.

3. **Break free from the data ghetto.** Many of us have invested in loyalty programs because they change customer behavior. But we can only influence behavior if we have some sort of

engagement and loyalty, and this begs the question: Are we really using our insights to transform the *entire* customer experience or just to drive sales? Instead of simply selling a product we should free our customer data across the organization to ensure that the experience is custom-made to the consumer's needs, from the in-box to the aisle.

4. **Be transparent and responsible.** The clearer you are about why you are requesting the information you seek, and how it will be used, the more reasonable the request will seem. In turn, the more likely your customer will be engaged with you. Being responsible also means limiting the amount of data you collect to only what you need, and then using that personal information in a way that benefits the consumer. We've seen that the customer's willingness to share his or her information with us goes up in direct proportion to his or her comfort level.

Achieving these principles will mean, in many cases, a wholesale change in corporate philosophy. But it will be worth it. Top-line growth is great, but we are often pawing blindly down the aisle without the consumer understanding that surrounds it, hoping that the next big promotion or campaign will lift sales above last year's numbers.

Without really knowing the person on the other end of that transaction, it will continue to be a guessing game.

ACKNOWLEDGMENTS

The ideas in this book have taken shape over many years and like any work in process, they are based on the talent and wisdom of the many people who have influenced me in so many ways. The book also would not have come to life had it not been for the patience and support of those closest to the project, both in the office and at home.

I have to start by thanking Jill McBride as the person who pushed me to stop just talking about a book and to actually start writing one. Jill's drive and enthusiasm for the project helped get it started and without her commitment to schedules and delivery timelines, this never would have been completed on time. Jill led the core team that brought this book to life from the book proposal stage to the very last edit. I also had the pleasure of working with a great writer for much of the book. Lisa Biank Fasig was a great writing partner. She was able to take my written work and our conversations and weave them into something that was interesting to read. Wardah Malik was a wonderful researcher and many times found a way to locate concrete references despite my obscure recollections of information. Finally, my assistant, Jocelyn Balluch, was critical to making sure everything was coordinated and she did a wonderful job of balancing my time commitments.

Behind the scenes, there were a number of colleagues who played important roles in making sure the ideas of the book were anchored in reality. Caroline Papadatos played a critical role in refining the manuscript and helping bring my ideas to life. Kelly Hlavinka and Jim Sullivan from our COLLOQUY publishing group provided ongoing support and helped frame out the book in the early stages. A number of LoyaltyOne associates were closely involved in bringing client examples to life so special thanks go out to Mitchell Merowitz, Miguel Pereira, Adrian Sosa, Brian Ross, Dennis Armbruster, Dino Di Pancrazio, Blair Cameron, Sharmane Good, Tim Lauber, and Jill Hickman for their help. Chris Houston provided added insights and support throughout the project and I thank him for his wise counsel. Nick Morgan of Public Words was instrumental in helping me develop a speech that brings *The Loyalty Leap* to life. Our sister company Epsilon is a leader in marketing services and my thanks go to both Bryan Kennedy and Taleen Ghazarian for their support and insight, as they brought additional dimension to many of the chapters.

In many ways, I would not have had the time to devote to the book without having a tremendous executive team to provide ongoing leadership at the company. My thanks go to Bruce Kerr, Todd March, Neil Everett, Stephanie Coyles, Bruce Burgetz, Dave Burns, Catherine McIntyre, Sofia Theodoreu, and Michael Kline for making sure we didn't miss a beat and for tolerating my book ambitions. I also must extend my thanks to Craig Underwood and John Scullion, the previous CEOs of our business. Both acted as mentors to me and I am a better leader and marketer today because of the many lessons I learned from them along the way.

At our parent company, Alliance Data Systems Corp., CEO Ed Heffernan provided me with great support to pursue my dream of writing this book. He has been a consistent source of encouragement as all of Alliance Data's divisions pursue our goals of a better marketing future for our clients. In addition, Karen Wald and the corporate marketing group have been a great support team on many items related to the book.

To the many LoyaltyOne clients who we have worked with for over two decades, entrusting us to help enrich their relationships and sharing their most interesting business problems: I can truly say thanks for the opportunities and the associated learning. To our international partners at Direxions in India and Dotz in Brazil: I look forward to growing together and sharing our knowledge as we build new experiences in these exciting economies.

Now that the book is finished, I'm grateful for the help and support of the team that is leading the marketing and public relations efforts, including Gillian Bagiamis, Jacob Younan, and the staff at JZMcBride and Associates.

At Penguin and Portfolio, my thanks go to Adrian Zackheim for believing in our ideas and agreeing to publish this book. Jillian Gray was a great editor and Will Weisser and his team provided marketing support. Andrea Magyar and the team at Penguin Canada were especially helpful and their advice and counsel were invaluable.

The book itself has been a journey but it's been more successful because we were able to work with one of the best book agents in the business—Jim Levine of Levine Greenberg. Jim and his team helped with the final book proposal, provided ongoing advice and counsel, and secured our global distribution with Penguin. As a new author, I can say Jim's industry knowledge, vast network of contacts, and mentoring were a huge help during the book development process. I can understand why he's such a great grandfather!

During the past year, I've had the opportunity to meet with other authors and have discovered an incredibly supportive and understanding group of people. Once you've gone through the "book process," it's like you are joining a club of like-experienced individuals. Thanks go to Simon Sinek, Jim Stengel, and Margo Krasne for their insights and guidance. A special thank-you goes to Mitch Joel, who beyond sharing his knowledge and experience has also been part psychotherapist through the entire process.

Most important, I must thank my family for their support and patience over the years. To my wife, Sally, and my kids, Jeremy, Robyn, and Hayley, I hope this book helps you understand how I've spent my time away from home. Despite the travel, long hours, and occasional interruptions during family vacations, I hope I've found a way to balance the two great passions in my life. I could not be any prouder of all of you!

NOTES

INTRODUCTION: From Customer Information to Customer Intimacy: What's Behind the Curtain?

1. Kelly Hlavinka and Jim Sullivan, "The Billion Member March: The COLLOQUY Loyalty Census," COLLOQUY white paper (April 2011).

CHAPTER 1: Four Forces Are Reshaping Marketing: Can You Ride the Wave of Change?

1. Interview with Alexis Nasard, chief commercial officer at Heineken, Interbrand—Best Global Brands 2010; www.interbrand.com/en/best-global-brands/Best-Global-Brands-2010/heineken-AlexisNasard.aspx.
2. Interview with José Parés, chief sales and marketing officer at Grupo Modelo, Interbrand—Best Global Brands 2010; www.interbrand.com/en/best-global-brands/Best-Global-Brands-2010/GRUPO-MODELO-PARES.aspx.
3. Paul Sutherland, "Colliding Stars Spark New Cosmic Blast," *Skymania: Astronomy and Space Guide*, May 24, 2007; www.skymania.com/wp/2007/05/colliding-stars-spark-new-cosmic-blast.html.

4. Marcia Reynolds, "Are You Wired to Skim Through Life?" *Wander Woman Blog*, January 29, 2011; www.psychologytoday.com/blog/wander-woman/201101/are-you-wired-skim-through-life.
5. Steve Ruble, "Use Your Scale to Cut a Path to Potential Consumers' Attention," *Ad Age Digital*, February 8, 2010; www/adage.com/article/steve-rubel/scale-cut-a-path-potential-consumers-attention/141949.
6. "Study: Multitasking Is Counterproductive," August 6, 2011; http://articles.cnn.com/2001-08-05/business/multitasking.study_1_cell-phone-researchers-tasks?_s=PM:CAREER.
7. Kaiser Family Foundation report, "Generation M^2: Media in the Lives of 8- to 18-Year-Olds" (January 2010); www.kff.org/entmedia/8010.cfm.
8. R. I. M. Dunbar, "Coevolution of Neocortical Size, Group Size and Language in Humans," *Behavioral and Brain Sciences* 16 no. 4 (1993): 681–735; www.radicalanthropologygroup.org/old/class_text_014.doc.
9. Jennifer Yang, "How a Tweet Sent Cineplex on a Bed Bug Scramble," *The Star*, August 31, 2010; www.thestar.com/news/gta/article/855193-how-twitter-got-the-tiff-bed-bug-story-wrong; Michael Posner, "The Tweet That Sent TIFF into a Bedbug Frenzy," *The Globe and Mail*, August 31, 2010; www.theglobeandmail.com/news/arts/tiff/the-tweet-that-sent-tiff-into-a-bedbug-frenzy/article1691242.
10. Martinne Geller, "P&G Dismisses DryMax Pampers Rash Rumors," Reuters, May 6, 2010; www.reuters.com/article/2010/05/07/us-procter-pampers-idUSTRE6457AH20100507.
11. "Broken guitar song gets airline's attention," CBC News, July 8, 2009; www.cbc.ca/news/arts/music/story/2009/07/08/united-breaks-guitars.html.
12. Nina Kruschwitz and Rebecca Shockley, "First Look: The Second Annual New Intelligence Enterprise Survey," *MIT Sloan Management Review*, June 22, 2011; www.sloanreview.mit.edu/the-magazine/2011-summer/52413/first-look-the-second-annual-new-intelligent-enterprise-survey.

CHAPTER 2: Privacy: Are We Really Going to $%@# This Up?

1. Jim Quail, editorial, *The Vancouver Sun*, August 30, 1996, p. A15.
2. "Data, Data Everywhere," *The Economist*, February 25, 2010; www.economist.com/node/15557443.
3. Ibid.
4. Brilliant Earth, "Gold Mining and the Environment," accessed November 21, 2011; www.brilliantearth.com/gold-mining-environment.
5. Laura Linkomies, ed., International Report, *Privacy Laws & Business*, no. 112, (September 2011).
6. Alexia Nielsen, "Advertising Option Icon Part 1: A Solution for Behavioral Targeting Privacy Concerns?" *Crowd Science*, August 9, 2011; www.blog.crowdscience.com/2011/08/advertising-option-icon-solution-behavioral-targeting-privacy-concerns.
7. Lawrence M. Kimmel, "Debate Room: Tracking Has a Plus Side," *Bloomberg BusinessWeek*; www.businessweek.com/debateroom/archives/2011/01/_pro_get_your_nose.html.
8. Kim Zetter, "Lawsuits Pour In Over Google's WiFi Data Collection," *Wired*, May 26, 2010; www.wired.com/threatlevel/2010/05/google-sued.
9. "Google breached Canada's privacy laws," CBCNews, October 19, 2010; www.cbc.ca/news/technology/story/2010/10/19/google-street-view-privacy.html.
10. David Murphy, "Google Abandons Street View in Germany," PCMag.com, April 10, 2011; www.pcmag.com/article2/0,2817,2383363,00.asp.
11. Ibid.
12. Joel Stein, "Data Mining: How Companies Now Know Everything About You," *Time*, March 10, 2011; www.time.com/time/business/article/0,8599,2058114,00.html.
13. Jacqui Cheng, "More Facebook Privacy Woes: Gay Users Outed to Advertisers," *Wired*, October 21, 2010.
14. Shar VanBoskirk, "Privacy Matters for Online Advertisers," Forrester Research report, September 21, 2010.

15. Bryan Pearson, "Challenges Marketers Face in a Privacy-Worried World," LoyaltyOne 2011 Research, United States and Canada (October 2011).
16. Poneman Institute, "2010 Most Trusted Companies for Privacy: U.S. Consumers," February 28, 2010.
17. Stein, "Data Mining."
18. "Pandora Accused of Collecting 'Mass Quantities' of Personal Data Via Mobile Apps," *MobileMarketingWatch*, April 8, 2011; www.mobilemarketingwatch.com/pandora-accused-of-collecting-mass-quantities-of-personal-data-via-mobile-apps-14433.
19. Stein, "Data Mining."
20. Matthew J. Schwartz, "Sony Sued Over PlayStation Network Hack," *Information Week*, April 27, 2011; www.informationweek.com/news/security/attacks/229402362.
21. "Tesco Vetoes Use of Loyalty Data for Healthy Eating Promo," *warc*; www.warc.com/Content/News/N14884_Tesco_Vetoes_Use_of_Loyalty_Data_for_Healthy_Eating_Promo.content?CID=N14884&ID=09fe8ea2-1303-47d9-96e7-8d7d42962508&q=snacks&qr=.
22. Rachel Barnes, "Tesco Refuses Government Clubcard Share Plan," *Marketing*, March 8, 2011; www.marketingmagazine.co.uk/sectors/governmentnonprofit/article/1058660/Tesco-refuses-government-Clubcard-share-plan.
23. Rob Pegoraro, "Facebook 'Sponsored Stories' Turn You into the Ad," *Washington Post*, January 27, 2011; www.voices.washingtonpost.com/fasterforward/2011/01/facebook_sponsored_stories_tur.html.
24. David Kravets, "Judge Approves $9.5 Million Facebook 'Beacon' Accord," *Wired*, March 17, 2010.
25. Byron Acohido, "Facebook Settles with FTC over Deception Charges," *USA Today*, November 30, 2011; www.usatoday.com/tech/news/story/2011-11-29/facebook-settles-with-ftc/51467448/1.
26. Mark Zuckerberg, "Our Commitment to the Facebook Community," *The Facebook Blog*, November 29, 2011; https://blog.facebook.com/blog.php?post=10150378701937131.
27. "Consumers Well Aware of Behavioral Tracking, Targeting—Don't

Like It Much," *MediaBuyerPlanner*; www.mediabuyerplanner.com/entry/34630/consumers-well-aware-of-behavioral-tracking-targeting-dont-like-it-much.

28. Miguel Helft, "Apple and Google Use Phone Data to Map the World," *New York Times*, April 25, 2011; www.nytimes.com/2011/04/26/technology/26locate.html?_r=2&ref=business.
29. Sara Jerome, "Google, Apple Questioned by House Republicans on Location Tracking," *Huffington Post*, April 26, 2011; www.huffingtonpost.com/2011/04/26/google-apple-questioned-on-location-tracking_n_853704.html; Miguel Helft and Kevin J. O'Brien, "Inquiries Grow Over Apple's Data Collection Processes," *New York Times*, April 21, 2011; www.nytimes.com/2011/04/22/technology/22data.html?partner=rss&emc=rss.
30. "Unsubscribe E-mails Strategy Report," Epsilon E-mail Institute, May 2011; www.emailinstitute.com/premium/unsubscribe-email-strategies-report.

CHAPTER 3: Making the Leap: How Do I Achieve Growth Through Customer Intimacy?

1. Michael Treacy and Fred Wiersema, *The Discipline of Market Leaders* (New York: Basic Books, 1997).
2. "The World's Most Innovative Companies 2011," *Fast Company* (2011); www.fastcompany.com/most-innovative-companies/2011/profile/apple.php.
3. Elaine Wong, "100-Calorie Packs Pack It In," *AdWeek*, May 26, 2009; www.adweek.com/news/advertising-branding/100-calorie-packs-pack-it-105846.
4. Elissa Gootman, "Seniors-Friendly Guide to Upper West Side Grocery Stores," *New York Times*, April 26, 2011; www.cityroom.blogs.nytimes.com/2011/04/26/seniors-friendly-guide-to-upper-west-side-grocery-stores/?ref=wholefoodsmarketinc.
5. "Whole Foods Market Company Information," *New York Times*

accessed November 22, 2011; http://topics.nytimes.com/top/news/business/companies/whole_foods_market_inc/index.html.

6. Win Weber, white paper report, "It's Time for the Turtles to Fly," GMA Forum (Mid-Winter 2007–8).
7. American Express, press release, "Good Service Is Good Business: American Consumers Willing to Spend More with Companies That Get Service Right, According to American Express Survey," May 3, 2011; http://about.americanexpress.com/news/pr/2011/csbar.aspx.
8. Peter Drucker, *The Practice of Management* (New York: Harper & Row, 1954), p. 37.
9. "Composing Your Life," *WeLoveAd* (2010); www.welovead.com/en/works/details/6a3BilsD.
10. Frederick F. Reichheld, "A Satisfied Customer Isn't Enough," Harvard Business School Press, March 6, 2006; www.theultimatequestion.com/theultimatequestion/tuq_article_detail.asp?groupCode=8&id=24313&menu_url=reviews.asp.
11. Net Promoter Web site; www.netpromoter.com/netpromoter_community/index.jspa.
12. Frederick F. Reichheld, *The Loyalty Effect: The Hidden Force Behind Growth, Profits, and Lasting Value* (Boston: Harvard Business Review Press, 2001).
13. Stephanie Coyles and Timothy C. Gokey, "Customer Retention Is Not Enough," *McKinsey Quarterly*, February 1, 2002.
14. Bill Doyle, *Customer Advocacy 2010: How Customers Rate US Banks, Investment Firms, and Insurers*, Forrester Research, January 29, 2010; www.forrester.com/rb/Research/customer_advocacy_2010_how_customers_rate_us/q/id/55483/t/2.
15. John H. Fleming and Jim Asplund, *Human Sigma: Managing the Employee-Customer Encounter* (New York: Gallup Press, 2007).
16. Ibid.

CHAPTER 4: Customer Loyalty Versus Customer Intimacy: Is There Really a Difference?

1. Kelly Hlavinka and Jim Sullivan, "The Billion Member March."
2. Douglas MacMillan, Brad Stone, and James Aley, "Zynga's Quest for Big-Spending Whales," *Bloomberg BusinessWeek*, July 7, 2011; www.bloomberg.com/news/2011-07-07/zynga-s-quest-for-big-spending-whales.html.
3. Terri Gaughan and Rick Ferguson, white paper report, "ValueTalk: The Great Value Proposition Debate" (November 2005).
4. Precima case study, for Alliance Data Systems. "Enterprise Customer Management," August 2006.

CHAPTER 5: The Four Doors to Relevance: What Are the Keys to Unlocking Opportunity?

1. Mark Vandenbosch and Kyle Murray, "Relevant by Design," Enterprise Loyalty in Practice, COLLOQUY, (Spring 2011).
2. Dan Butcher, "McDonald's LBS mobile ads achieve 7 percent click through rate," *Mobile Commerce Today*, April 14, 2010; www.mobilecommercedaily.com/2010/04/14/mcdonalds-lbs-mobile-ads-achieve-7-percent-ctr.
3. "What's Next For Geolocation? Apps, Apps, Apps," *ReadWriteWeb*, February 8, 2010; www.readwriteweb.com/archives/whats_next_for_geolocation_apps_apps_apps.php.
4. Marissa McNaughton, "US Mobile Internet Use to Increase 25%, Smartphone Use Nearly 50% in 2011," The Realtime Report, August 26, 2011; http://therealtimereport.com/2011/08/26/us-mobile-internet-use-to-increase-25-smartphone-use-nearly-50-in-2011.
5. Press release, IDG Global Solutions, "IDG Global Survey Shows Smartphone Use Growing Rapidly with Regional Differences," July 11, 2011; www.marketwatch.com/story/idg-global-survey-shows-smartphone-use-growing-rapidly-with-regional-differences-2011-07-11.

6. Epsilon Targeting, report, "New Mover Report 2010: Capturing the Window of Opportunity," July 2010; www.epsilon.com/pr/NewMover 2010.
7. Hoang Nguyen, "An Analysis on Best Buy's Customer-Centric Innovation," Bukisa.com, November 14, 2010 (posted); www.bukisa.com/articles/395115_an-analysis-on-best-buys-customer-centric-innova tion; COLLOQUY Enterprise Loyalty Scan (subscriber only). March 10, 2010.
8. Best Buy Form 10K (annual report), fiscal year 2010 and fiscal year 2011.
9. Bill Brohaugh, "2011 COLLOQUY Loyalty Summit Highlight Films: The NHL Goes into Customer-Relationship Overtime," COLLOQUY, September 14, 2011; http://blog.colloquy.com/2011/09/14/2011-colloquy-loyalty-summit-highlight-films-the-nhl-goes-into-customer-relation ship-overtime.
10. Donnel Briley and Jennifer Aaker, "When Does Culture Matter? Effects of Personal Knowledge on the Correction of Culture-Based Judgments," *Journal of Marketing Research,* published August 1, 2006; www.marketingpower.com/AboutAMA/Pages/AMA%20Publi cations/AMA%20Journals/Journal%20of%20Marketing%20Research/TOCs/SUM_2006.3/When_Does_Culture_Matter.aspx. Also: www.gsb.stanford.edu/news/research/mktg_aaker_cultureinfluences.shtml.

CHAPTER 6: Turning Fear on Its Ear: Can You Inspire Loyalty Through Hope?

1. Robert A. Schwartz, "Skin Cancer: Recognition and Management," *Journal of the American Medical Association* (September 3, 2008).
2. Sun-Protection-and-Products-Guide.com, www.sun-protection-and-products-guide.com/famous-people-with-skin-cancer.html; "Celebrities & Skin Cancer," *HealthKey,* www.healthkey.com/health/physical-conditions/death/sns-health-skin-cancer-celebs,0,6666652.story; "TV's Philbin reports his own skin cancer on today's 'Live with Regis

& Kathie Lee Show,'" *PRNewswire*, June 1, 1990, www.highbeam.com/doc/1G1-8497896.html.

3. Samantha Critchell, "Celebrities shun sun for skin cancer awareness," *USAToday*, April 15, 2008; www.usatoday.com/weather/climate/2008-04-15-skin-cancer_N.htm.
4. "Brandy, Tatyana Ali & Danielle Fishel Get Naked for Cancer Campaign," StarPulse.com, May 17, 2011; www.starpulse.com/news/index.php/2011/05/17/brandy_tatyana_ali_danielle_fishel_ge.
5. "Sunscreen Sales Have Room to Grow," *Household and Personal Products Industry*, February 15, 2010; www.happi.com/news/2010/02/15/sunscreen_sales_have_room_to_grow.
6. Elizabeth Olson, "The Rub on Sunscreen," *New York Times*, June 19, 2009; www.nytimes.com/2006/06/19/health/healthspecial/19sun.html?pagewanted=print.
7. Staff report, *Shore News Today*, June 24, 2011.
8. Toni Clarke, "Pfizer wins Viagra patent battle against Teva," Reuters, August 15, 2011; www.reuters.com/article/2011/08/15/pfizer-idUSN1E77E06B20110815.
9. "Antibacterial Product Fears," CBS New York, Daily Finance August 10, 2010; http://newyork.cbslocal.com/2010/08/10/seen-at-11-antibacterial-product-fears.
10. "Tontine Wins Grand Effie, Clems Melbourne Named Most Effective Agency," *B&T*, August 26, 2011; www.bandt.com.au/news/tontine-wins-grand-effie-clems-melbourne-named-mo.
11. Jennifer Alsever, "Bedbug invasion is turning into big business," MSNBC, October 11, 2010.
12. John Adams, "Two in Five Consumers Believe Mobile Banking Is Unsafe," *American Banker*, July 20, 2011.
13. Michael Silverstein and Neil Fiske, *Trading Up: The New American Luxury* (New York: Portfolio, 2003), p. 67.
14. "lululemon athletica inc. Announces Fourth Quarter and Full Year Fiscal 2010 Results," *Business Wire*, March 17, 2011; www.investor.lululemon.com/releasedetail.cfm?ReleaseID=558393.
15. Hilary Oliver, "Echinacea study no death knell for supplement," *Natu-*

ral Foods Merchandiser, April 24, 2008; www.newhope360.com/botanicals/echinacea-study-no-death-knell-supplement.

16. Press release, "Most Women 'Feel Good' Being Philanthropic, but Want Convenient Ways of Donating: Seven in Ten Prefer Supporting Causes through Everyday Purchases," Ipsos, May 18, 2011.
17. *Top 10 UK Dating Sites*; www.top10ukdatingsites.co.uk/top-10-by-rating.
18. Douglas Quenqua, "With Enough Soldiers, the Army Is Looking for a Few Good Officers," *New York Times*, August 2, 2009.

CHAPTER 7: Enterprise Loyalty: What Defines the Customer Experience?

1. Martin Hilbert and Priscila López, "The World's Technological Capacity to Store, Communicate, and Compute Information," *Science* Express (February 10, 2011): 60–65.
2. "Confirmation Bias," *Dictionary of Psychology*; www.dictionary-psychology.com/index.php?a=term&d=Dictionary+of+psychology&t=Confirmation+bias.
3. Form 10-K (2010 annual report), Caesars Entertainment Corp., March 4, 2011.
4. KPMG Advisory, *Harrah's: A Customer Relationship Management Case Study*, 2006.
5. Caesars Entertainment, private company report, "An Emergent Model in a Recovering Industry," 2011 UBS Leveraged Finance Conference, May 2011.
6. COLLOQUY Staff, "Mapping the Customer Journey," *Enterprise Loyalty in Practice,* (Fall 2010).
7. Ibid.
8. Dana Flavelle, "RONA Sees Growth in Canadian Market," *Toronto Star*, April 27, 2011.
9. "Target to Open 'CityTarget' on Chicago's State Street," *Minneapolis/St. Paul Business Journal*, February 15, 2011.

10. COLLOQUY Staff, "From Hypothesis to Insight to Action," *Enterprise Loyalty in Practice* (Spring 2011).
11. Woolworths South Africa, 5One presentation, National Retail Federation Big Show annual convention, 2008.
12. Brian Ross, "The Assortment Opportunity," *Enterprise Loyalty in Practice* (Spring 2011).
13. Case study, "Priority Shoppers: Ready for Their Close-Up," *Precima* (May 2010).
14. COLLOQUY Staff, "The COLLOQUY Loyalty Rewards" 18 (5) *COLLOQUY*, December 3, 2010.
15. Natalie Zmuda, "Coca-Cola's Futuristic Soda Fountain to Get 2012 Ad Push," *Advertising Age*, August 8, 2011; www.adage.com/article/news/coca-cola-s-futuristic-soda-fountain-2012-ad-push/229154.

CHAPTER 8: Employee Loyalty: How Do I Build a Customer-Centric Culture?

1. Megan Burns, Harley Manning, and Jennifer Peterson "The State of Customer Experience, 2011," Forrester Research (February 2011).
2. James L. Heskett et al., "Putting the Service-Profit Chain to Work," *Harvard Business Review* (July–August 2008).
3. Lisa Biank Fasig, "My Macy's Learns to Walk in Chicago Shoes," *Cincinnati Business Courier*, September 21, 2009.
4. Donald Sull, "10 Clues to Opportunity," *Strategy + Business*, August 23, 2011; www.strategy-business.com/article/11304?pg=all.
5. "Data Points: Finding Shoppers Where They Live," *Strategy + Business*, August 23, 2011; www.strategy-business.com/article/11314?gko=05216.
6. Geoff Kirbyson, "Frequent Grocery Fliers Get 'Elite' Status," *Winnipeg Free Press*, July 3, 2011.
7. Jena McGregor, "USAA's Battle Plan," *Bloomberg BusinessWeek*, February 18, 2010.
8. "Call Center Industry 2010 Award Winners for VoC Excellence"; www.sqmgroup.com/2010-call-center-award-winners.

9. "Memory Maker," (13) *HR Management*; www.hrmreport.com/article/Memory-maker; Matthew Smith and Derek Irvine, "The Power of Fairmont Hotels & Resorts' Strategic Employee Recognition Program," *WorkSpan*, August 2009.
10. Matas press release, "Matas announces Denmark's most beautiful app," July 25, 2011; www.translate.google.com/translate?hl=en&sl=da&u=http://www.matas.dk/om%2Bmatas/presse/2010/clubmatas.aspx&ei=VS1uTqGSCdGJsALnnpGtBA&sa=X&oi=translate&ct=result&resnum=3&ved=0CCsQ7gEwAg&prev=/search%3Fq%3D%2522Anne%2BLene%2BHamann%2522%2Bmatas%26hl%3Den%26client%3Dfirefox-a%26sa%3DN%26rls%3Dorg.mozilla:en-US:official%26biw%3D1188%26bih%3D713%26prmd%3Divnso.
11. Matas press release, "Danish women flocking to the customer club," December 15, 2010; www.translate.google.com/translate?hl=en&sl=da&u=http://www.matas.dk/om%2Bmatas/presse/2010/clubmatas.aspx&ei=VS1uTqGSCdGJsALnnpGtBA&sa=X&oi=translate&ct=result&resnum=3&ved=0CCsQ7gEwAg&prev=/search%3Fq%3D%2522Anne%2BLene%2BHamann%2522%2Bmatas%26hl%3Den%26client%3Dfirefox-a%26sa%3DN%26rls%3Dorg.mozilla:en-US:official%26biw%3D1188%26bih%3D713%26prmd%3Divnso.
12. Matas press release, "Club Matas at winning stool," May 6, 2011; www.translate.google.com/translate?hl=en&sl=da&u=http://www.matas.dk/om%2Bmatas/presse/2010/clubmatas.aspx&ei=VS1uTqGSCdGJsALnnpGtBA&sa=X&oi=translate&ct=result&resnum=3&ved=0CCsQ7gEwAg&prev=/search%3Fq%3D%2522Anne%2BLene%2BHamann%2522%2Bmatas%26hl%3Den%26client%3Dfirefox-a%26sa%3DN%26rls%3Dorg.mozilla:en-US:official%26biw%3D1188%26bih%3D713%26prmd%3Divnso.
13. Claire Swedberg, "Clothing Designer Brings RFID to Its Shoppers," *RFID Journal*, December 5, 2008.

CHAPTER 9: I Call, I Tweet—but How Do I Use Communications to Complete the Customer Experience?

1. Kelly Hlavinka, "Managing Those Pesky 'Madvocates' at United Airlines," *COLLOQUY Blog*, July 27, 2007; www.blog.colloquy.com/2011/07/27/managing-those-pesky-madvocates-at-united-airlines.
2. "The 50 Worst Cars of All Time," *Time Specials* (2007); www.time.com/time/specials/2007/0,28757,1658545,00.html.
3. *Car Design Online*, www.cardesignonline.com/design/modelling/index.php.
4. Gartner Inc., Research Methodologies abstract, "Magic Quadrants, Positioning Technology Players Within a Specific Market"; www.gartner.com/technology/research/methodologies/research_mq.jsp.
5. Phaedra Hise, "Loyalty Calling: Are Cell Phone Companies Finally Dialing the Right Numbers?" 19 (3) *COLLOQUY*, July 29, 2011.
6. Online definition of unstructured data, SearchBusinessAnalytics.com; searchbusinessanalytics.techtarget.com/definition/unstructured-data.
7. Cone LLC, *2010 Consumer New Media Study* (November 2010).
8. "FAQ page," *In the Chat*; www.inthechat.com/faq.aspx.
9. Pete Blackshaw, "What Best Buy Learned About Service as Marketing and Empowering Employees," *AdAge Digital*, November 24, 2009; www.adage.com/article/digital-columns/digital-marketing-buy-s-customer-service-twelpforce/140708.
10. Sharon M. Goldman, "Trialogue: The Intersection of Social Media and Loyalty," 19 (1) *COLLOQUY* (2011).
11. "The Value of a Facebook Fan: An Empirical Review," Syncapse and Hotspex Market Research (June 2010).
12. "Aerodynamics," *Car Design Online*; www.cardesignonline.com/design/aerodynamics/index.php.
13. Company award submission, Indigo Books, 2011 COLLOQUY Loyalty Awards, 2011.
14. "Deploying Social Media to Cultivate Customer Loyalty: A Benchmark Study," Direct Marketing Association and *COLLOQUY* (2010).

CHAPTER 10: How Do We Take the "Pry" Out of Privacy?

1. Bryan Pearson, "Challenges Marketers Face in a Privacy-Worried World," LoyaltyOne 2011 Research, United States and Canada (October 2011).
2. Ibid.
3. "Protecting Consumer Privacy in an Era of Rapid Change: A Proposed Framework for Businesses and Policymakers," Preliminary FTC Staff report, Federal Trade Commission (December 2010).
4. Pearson, "Challenges Marketers Face."
5. Ibid.

EPILOGUE

1. Marshall McLuhan, *Understanding Media: The Extensions of Man* (New York: McGraw Hill, 1964; reissued MIT Press, 1994, with introduction by Lewis H. Lapham; reissued by Gingko Press, 2003).

INDEX